The Power Drill Grammar Book

The Power Drill Grammar Book

By John & Alison Kooistra

Illustrations by Cynthia DiSimone

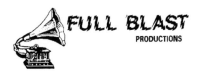

FULL BLAST PRODUCTIONS

IN CANADA   IN THE UNITED STATES

FB Productions   FB Productions
Box 408   Box 1297
Virgil, Ontario   Lewiston, New York 14092-8297
L0S 1T0

Canadian Cataloguing in Publication Data

Kooistra, John Peter, 1953-
   The power drill grammar book

ISBN 1-895451-35-3

1. English Language -- Grammar -- Problems,
exercises, etc. -- Juvenile literature.
I. Kooistra, Alison, 1979-   .
II. DiSimone, Cynthia, 1959-   . III. Title.

PE1112.K664 1999   428.2' 076   C00-930049-X

Illustrations by Cynthia DiSimone

Printed in Canada.

ISBN 1-895451-35-3

The Power Drill Grammar Book

Introduction

What makes the Power Drill Grammar Book unique?
It's fun. It's practical. The sample sentences are in step with modern times, and the grammar is a good mix of old school and modern theory. Most importantly, the Power Drills are focussed on students' primary needs -- error correction of their speech and writing in the formal register, and expansion of their range of expression.

Grammar instruction is important, but it is not the primary factor in the development of literacy skills. Most well-spoken, well-educated university graduates would have difficulty simply naming the parts of speech, and yet these students have an implicit and accurate grasp of thousands of complex grammar rules. Similarly, five-year-olds who can communicate effectively with their parents already have an implicit and accurate grasp of hundreds of grammatical concepts which neither they nor their parents could give a name to.

Many grammar drill books in actual fact do very little to aid students in the comprehension and enjoyment of their native or second language. These books focus too often on the naming of parts, and too often they offer confusing definitions. A classic example is the confident definition of the verb as "the word that describes the action in a sentence." This definition leaves out verbs such as BE and HAVE, and also leaves out most of the complexities of auxiliary verbs.

A way around these problems is to follow these precepts:

1. Use grammar terminology only when it is necessary.
2. Use this terminology accurately, and always keep it as simple as possible.
3. Focus grammar drills on practical problems relating to formal correctness, or the kind of error correction that will augment success rates in students' academic careers.
4. Always, make the drills as interesting and enjoyable as possible. Grammar should be the most enjoyable, not the least enjoyable, of your subjects.
5. Finally, keep in mind that the most important factor in the development of writing skills -- even more important than exercises of the kind found in this book -- is the amount of reading your students do. Teachers should, above all, be interested in increasing the number of occasions in which they may immerse (but not drown!) their students in the pure joys of reading and writing.

A few suggestions to teachers:

1. Several exercises in the Power Drill book ask students to write yes or no in the blanks beside sentences. For fun, use substitute phrases or pictures. For "yes", students could draw happy faces, or use whatever terms are currently popular ("cool", "awesome", etc.). For "No": a sad face, or "uncool", etc.

2. Relate as many lessons to the students' own lives as you can. Use names and examples from their immediate community.

3. Have students work on their answers in teams. Each team passes their work to another team to be marked, while you announce the correct answers. This gives immediate feedback, helps the students to teach each other, saves you a load of marking, and makes a bit of fun.

4. Each unit has a "Grammar Games" lesson which focuses on fun and challenges. Take a lead from these lessons (9, 19, etc.), and incorporate other fun activities into the earlier drills, or apply the same games, such as "I Spy," "Crazy Sentences," and "Guess the Adverb."

Table of Contents

Name: _____

Lesson 1 -- Sentences

Date: _____

How do people talk to each other?
We shout, we mumble, we grunt, we grumble.
Sometimes we use one word, like "no" or "yes" or "maybe".
Usually, though, we use full sentences.

Most sentences are groups of words that tell us something.
They usually have three parts: a beginning, a verb, and an ending.

	(beginning)	(verb)	(ending)
(a)	Amber	walked	to the mall.
(b)	She	bought	a mood ring.
(c)	Her mother	is	the President of the United States.

Write **Yes** before each line that is a complete sentence.
Write **No** before each line that is not a complete sentence.

_____ 1. Jason likes to play soccer.

_____ 2. Tiffany's favorite video game.

_____ 3. You walked to the mall with Amber.

_____ 4. my CD player.

_____ 5. Let's play with.

_____ 6. Dana has a little sister.

_____ 7. Dogs can be scary.

Take one line from the above list that is not a whole sentence.
Now, make a whole sentence out of it.
For example,"my CD player" is not a sentence, but it could be at the beginning of a whole
sentence or at the end of one.
"My CD player is broken."   "I love my CD player."

(a) _____

UNIT ONE   Name: _____

Lesson 2 -- Verbs   Date: _____

(a) A verb is usually a word that shows **action**. It shows what someone or something **does**.
(b) A verb can also show what someone or something **is**.
(c) A verb can also show what someone or something **has**.

Some verbs show **action**:
    buy, fight, run, play, eat, comb, sing, act, laugh....

Some verbs show what someone or something **is**:
    am, are, is, equals, looks like....

Some verbs show what someone or something **has**:
    has, have, owns, possess....

Find the verbs in the following sentences. Draw a circle around each verb.

1. You only comb your hair on picture day!

2. Ziggy bought a calculator for math class.

3. Anna sings along with her favorite radio station.

4. Poppy has five pairs of shoes.

5. Denise owns a Collector's Beanie Baby.

6. Zoe eats pizza every Friday night.

7. I am a bit sad today.

8. That cloud looks like my Aunt Selma.

    Now, make your own sentence using an **action** verb:

1. _____ .

    Make your own sentence using a verb showing what someone or something **is**:

2. _____ .

    Make your own sentence using a verb showing what someone or something **has**:

3. _____ .

Name: _____

Lesson 3 -- Verbs

Date: _____

Use each of these verbs in a sentence. Draw a circle around each verb.

fight   run   play   eat   comb   sing   laugh

am, are, is   equals   looks like

has, have   own

Example: (Use *fight, fights,* or *fought*)
Donny fights with his brothers about what to watch on television.

1. *(Use run, runs,* or *ran)* :_____

_____

2. *(Use play, plays,* or *played)* :_____

_____

3. *(Use eat, eats,* or *ate)* :_____

_____

4. *(comb, combs,* or *combed)* :_____

_____

5. *(sing, sings,* or *sang)* :_____

_____

6. *(am, are, is, was,* or *were)* :_____

_____

7. *(equal, equals,* or *equalled)* :_____

_____

8. *(look like, looks like,* or *looked like)* :_____

_____

9. *(has, have,* or *had)* :_____

_____

10. *(own, owns,* or *owned)* :_____

_____

Lesson 4a — Past. Present. Future.   Date: _____

> The past.   Sentences can describe yesterday, or last week, or last year.
>
> The present time.   Sentences can describe something about today, or right now.
>
> The future.   Sentences can describe tomorrow, or next week, or next year.

We change the verbs in our sentences to show the past, the present and the future. Here are two charts showing **a few** of the changes we can make.

	Past	Present	Future	of the verb **be**
I	was	am	will be	
You (one person)	were	are	will be	
She (or He, or It)	was	is	will be	
We, You (plural), They	were	are	will be	

	Past	Present	Future	of the verb **have**
I	had	have	will have	
You (one person)	had	have	will have	
She (or He, or It)	had	has	will have	
We, You (plural), They	had	have	will have	

A.   Finish these sentences about yourself, using the verb **have**.

1. When I was little, _____.

2. Today, _____.

3. When I grow up, _____.

B.   Finish these sentences about yourself, using the verb **be**.

1. Yesterday, I _____.
                (happy? sad? crazy? tired? angry? excited?)

2. Today, I _____.
                (happy? sad? crazy? tired? angry? excited?)

3. Tomorrow, I _____.
                (happy? sad? crazy? tired? angry? excited?)

Name: _____

Lesson 4b — Past. Present. Future.   Date: _____

The past. Sentences can describe what happened yesterday, or last week, or last year.

The present time. Sentences can describe what is happening today, or right now.

The future. Sentences can describe what will happen tomorrow, or next week, or next year.

We change the verbs in our sentences to show the past, the present and the future. This little chart shows **a few** of the changes we can make.

Past	Present (two forms)	Future
liked	(I) like, (He/She/It) likes	will like
bought	(I) buy, (He/She/It) buys	will buy
looked	(I) look, (He/She/It) looks	will look
combed	(I) comb, (He/She/It) combs	will comb
ate	(I) eat, (He/She/It) eats	will eat
played	(I) play, (He/She/It) plays	will play

A.   Finish these sentences about yourself, using the verb **like**.

1. When I was little, _____.

2. Today, _____.

3. When I grow up, _____.

B.   Finish these sentences about a friend (or brother, or sister), using the verb **like**.

1. When he/she was little, _____.

2. Today, _____.

3. When he/she grows up, _____.

C.   Finish these sentences about yourself, using the verb **play**.

1. When I was little, _____.

2. Today, _____.

3. When I grow up, _____.

Name: _____

Lesson 5 — Past. Present. Future.   Date: _____

Past. Sentences can describe what happened yesterday, last week, or last year.
Present. Sentences can describe what is happening today, or right now.
Future. Sentences can describe what will happen tomorrow, or next week, or next year.

Teacher: divide your students into small groups.
1.   (a) Each student in the group will describe one funny thing that happened yesterday.
       (b) Each one of you will write the sentence you liked best in the space below. You can
             write down the sentence you made up, or someone else's sentence.
       (c) Each student will underline the verb.

(Example: Yesterday, I <u>spilled</u> orange juice on the cat.)

Yesterday, _____

2. Each student in the group will describe one scary thing that happened last week. Next,
write the sentence you liked best in the space below, and underline the verb.

(Example: Last week, my neighbor's dog <u>chased</u> me down the street.)

Last week, _____

3. Each student in the group will describe one interesting thing that happens every day.
Then, write the sentence you liked best in the space below, and underline the verb.

(Example: Every day, my brother <u>makes</u> a goofy face in the mirror.)

Every day, _____

4. Each student in the group will describe one bad thing that happens every day. Then, write
the sentence you liked best in the space below. Underline the verb.

(Example: Every day, I <u>wake up</u> way too early.)

Every day, _____

5. Each student in the group will describe one fun thing they will definitely do next
weekend. Then, write the sentence you liked best in the space below. Underline the verb(s).

(Example: Next weekend, I <u>will</u> <u>go</u> <u>camping</u> with my family.)

Next weekend, _____

Name: _____

Lesson 6 -- Capital Letters   Date: _____

Small letters: a b c d e f g h i j k l m n o p q r s t u v w x y z
Capital letters: A B C D E F G H I J K L M N O P Q R S T U V W X Y Z

When do we use capital letters?
(a) The first word in every sentence begins with a capital letter.
(b) The word "I" *is* a capital letter. (Example: **M**y father says that **I** watch too much TV.)
(c) The names of people and pets begin with capital letters.
(d) The names of stores and businesses begin with capital letters (like the companies that
      make clothes, movies, music, cars, and so on).

A. **W**rite down the names of three people that you know. Write their first names and their
last names, and underline the capital letters.

Example: **M** o e s h a **C** l a r k

1. _____
2. _____
3. _____

Use one of these names in a sentence. (Example: **Moesha Clark is my best friend.**)

4. _____ .

B. Write down the names of three pets that you know about. They can be your own pets, or
pets that you know from TV shows, or your friends' pets. (Don't forget to use capital letters,
or you might hurt the pets' feelings!)

1. _____
2. _____
3. _____

Use one of these names in a sentence.

4. _____ .

C. Write down the names of three companies that you know about. These companies can
make clothes, cars, perfume, running shoes, food, and so on.

1. _____
2. _____
3. _____

Use one of these names in a sentence.

4. _____ .

Lesson 7 -- Capital Letters   Date: _____

Small letters: a b c d e f g h i j k l m n o p q r s t u v w x y z
Capital letters: A B C D E F G H I J K L M N O P Q R S T U V W X Y Z

Think of two examples for each category.

1. (a) days, (b) months, (c) holidays

(a) Examples of days: <u>Wednesday</u> and <u>Friday</u>.

_____   _____

(b) Examples of months: <u>August</u> and <u>February</u>.

_____   _____

(c) Examples of holidays: <u>Hallowe'en</u> and <u>Thanksgiving</u>.

_____   _____

2. Titles of respect

For example: <u>Princess Diana</u>, <u>Judge Judy</u>, <u>Mr. Knowles</u>, and <u>Senator Brown</u>.

_____   _____

3. Names (a) of people (b) of places (c) of groups (like teams or companies or bands)

(a) Examples of names: <u>Martha</u>, <u>Pedro</u>, and <u>Sandra</u>.

_____   _____

(b) Examples of places: <u>Tallahassee</u>, the <u>Epcot Center</u>, <u>Pizza Palace</u>, and <u>Jamaica</u>.

_____   _____

(c) Examples of teams, companies, bands: <u>Chicago Bears</u>, <u>Pepsi-Cola</u>, and <u>The Beatles</u>.

_____   _____

Name: _____

Lesson 8 -- Capital Letters

Date: _____

The names of special places begin with capital letters. Special places include the names of countries, states or provinces, cities, rivers, baseball stadiums, hockey arenas, movie theaters, malls and schools.

Add two names to each list.

Mexico, United States, Canada.

1. _____ 2. _____

California, Florida, Ohio, North Dakota, Ontario, Alberta, Quebec.

1. _____ 2. _____

Chicago, Los Angeles, Toronto.

1. _____ 2. _____

Mississippi River, Niagara River.

1. _____ 2. _____

Yankee Stadium, Wrigley Field, Madison Square Garden.

1. _____ 2. _____

The Roxy Theater, Cineplex Odeon.

1. _____ 2. _____

Fairview Mall, The Galleria, Bloomingdales.

1. _____ 2. _____

Washington Public School, J. A. Macdonald High School.

1. _____ 2. _____

Lesson 9 -- The Grammar Games!   Date: _____

1. "I Spy...."

Take turns. Nine students in the class have a chance to name something in the class that begins with a capital letter (name of student, name of shoe, name of teacher). The student has to say, "I see a person or a thing that begins with the letter ___?___ ." Everyone in the class has to guess what the answer is and then write each new word in the blanks below.

_____   _____   _____

_____   _____   _____

_____   _____   _____

2. "I Spied...."

Eight students in the class have a chance to name a show they saw last week on TV. Each student has to say, "Last week, I saw a TV show that begins with the letter _____ ." Everyone in the class has to guess what the answer is and then write each new word in the blanks below.

_____   _____

_____   _____

_____   _____

_____   _____

3. "I Will Spy...."

Eight students in the class have a chance to name a video or a video game which they will watch or play sometime next week. Each student has to say, "Next week, I will watch a video (or play a video game) that begins with the letter _____ ." Everyone in the class has to guess what the answer is and then write each new word in the blanks below.

_____   _____

_____   _____

_____   _____

_____   _____

{Note to teacher: you should repeat this game, with variations, for other grammatical items: e.g., spy the noun, etc.}

Name: _____

Date: _____

A.   Write **Yes** before each line that is a complete sentence.
Write **No** before each line that is not a complete sentence.
Also, draw a circle around the verb in each sentence.

_____   1. Tiffany likes to.

_____   2. Jason's favorite video game is Pod Racer.

_____   3. wrecked my video game controller.

_____   4. Conchita enjoys chocolate.

_____   5. Very big dogs with big teeth can do.

B.   Circle the correct form of the verb in each sentence.

1. Yesterday, Jorge **ran / runs / will run** all the way home.

2. Next weekend, Tonya **sang / sings / will sing** her favorite song at the karaoke party.

3. Most of the time, Jackson **looks like / is looking like / will look like** his older brother.

4. Every time you add them up, 75 plus 75 **equalled / is equalling / equals** 150.

5. Last year, Albert **ate / eats / will eat** a chocolate bar for lunch every single day.

6. This coming year, Albert **ate / eats / will eat** a granola bar for lunch every single day.

C.   Write down the names of three movie or television stars.
Write their first names and their last names, and underline the capital letters.

Example: <u>W</u>ill <u>S</u>mith

1. _____

2. _____

3. _____

D.   Fun Bonus. Write **your** names backwards (remember to use capital letters properly).
If your name is "Gord Parsons", you will write it as "Drog Snosrap".

_____

What does your new name make you think of?
What kind of character would "Drog Snosrap" play in a movie?

Name: _____

Lesson 11 — Question Sentences   Date: _____

Most sentences are groups of words that **tell** us something.
Other sentences are **questions** — groups of words that **ask** us something.
Many questions begin with verbs such as

Do   Does   Did   Is   Are   Have   Will

The answers to these questions usually start with a simple **Yes** or **No**.

A.   Draw a happy face before each line that is a question.
        Draw a sad face before each line that is **not** really a whole question.

_____   1. Does Jason like to play football?

_____   2. Is Pokémon Tiffany's favorite video game?

_____   3. Did you visit the?

_____   4. Does Rashid love his CD player?

_____   5. A sound card on your computer?

_____   6. Your favorite team last year the Yankees?

_____   7. Will Moesha make the basketball team?

B.   Answer two of the good, whole questions above with whole sentences. Start your
        sentences with "Yes" or "No".

Example. Question: Will Moesha make the basketball team?
          Answer: Yes, Moesha will definitely make the team.

1. _____

2. _____

C.   Take two lines from the above list that are not whole questions.
        Now, fix them. Turn them into complete questions.

3. _____

4. _____

Name: _____

Lesson 12 — Questions

Date: _____

Most sentences are groups of words that TELL us something.
Other sentences are **questions** — groups of words that ASK us something.
Many questions begin with words such as

Why   When   Where   Who   How

The answers to these questions give us information.

A.   Draw a happy face before each line that is a question.
           Draw a sad face before each line that is not really a whole question.

_____   1. Where does Mario?

_____   2. Why is Pokémon the game that Tiffany?

_____   3. How did you get to the mall yesterday?

_____   4. When did Rashid buy his DVD player?

_____   5. Who bought a sound card for her computer?

_____   6. When did the Yankees?

_____   7. How well did Moesha play during the practice?

B.   Answer two of the questions with whole sentences.

Example. Question: How well did Moesha play during the practice?
              Answer: Moesha played some very good basketball.

1. _____

2. _____

C.   Take two lines from the above list that are not whole questions.
           Now, fix them. Turn them into complete questions.

3. _____

4. _____

Lesson 13 — Nouns

What is a noun? The word "noun" is like the word "name".

A **noun** is a word that names a **person**, **place**, or **thing**.

Jakamo bought a huge television in Dallas.

Jakamo is the name of a person.
Television is the name of a thing.
Dallas is the name of a place.

A. Put a line under the noun in each sentence.
At the end of each sentence, write **person**, **place**, or **thing**.

Example:
My <u>skates</u> are way too small.   _____thing_____

1. Jeremy is very noisy.   _____

2. Yellowstone Park is really beautiful.   _____

3. Where is Canada located?   _____

4. The VCR isn't working right now.   _____

5. Lateesha dances very well.   _____

6. The pizza is late.   _____

7. That car is truly powerful.   _____

8. Will Tyrone play next week?   _____

B. Now make up three sentences of your own using a different kind of noun each time:

1. _____ .   ____person____

2. _____ .   ____place____

3. _____ .   ____thing____

Name: _____

Lesson 14 — Nouns

Date: _____

A **noun** is a word that names a **person**, **place**, or **thing**.

A.   All of the sentences below have more than one noun. Draw a line under each noun.

1. Dad is making eggs for lunch.

2. Ms. Lansdowne marks the students' homework.

3. Joe downloaded this game from the Internet.

4. Brittany and Brooklyn are shopping for new shoes.

5. Many bands come from Seattle.

6. Mr. Tachito owns a sporty red car.

7. My grandpa is going to take me to the big game.

8. Mrs. Pewters likes to eat fries with gravy.

9. Alex is climbing the tree behind her house.

10. My mom wants to buy me new clothes for school.

B.   Make up two of your own sentences using at least one word from each of the three lists below. You get extra points if you can use more than one word from each list.

Persons: Kareem, Jody, Kevin, Lisa, Maria, mother, father, people, student....
Places: New York, Seattle, California, park, school, mall, record store....
Things: jeans, dog, wallet, watch, skateboard, roller blades, purse, earrings....

Example: Kareem lost his wallet in New York.

Your sentences: 1. _____

_____.

2. _____

_____.

Name: _____

Lesson 15 — Pronouns

Date: _____

A **pronoun** is a word that is used in the place of a noun.

This paragraph does not have any pronouns in it.

> Tony practices on **Tony's** guitar every day. **Tony's** mother told **Tony** that **Tony** is getting very good. **Tony** wants to play in **Tony's** father's rock band next year.

This new version is better because it uses pronouns.

> Tony practices on **his** guitar every day. **His** mother told **him** that **he** is getting very good. **He** wants to play in **his** father's rock band next year.

There are many kinds of pronouns. These are the ones we use the most.

	SINGULAR					PLURAL		
1.	I	you	she	he	it	we	you	they
2.	me	you	her	him	it	us	you	them
3.	my	your	her	his	its	our	your	their
4.	mine	yours	hers	his		ours	yours	theirs

Row #1 gives pronouns that usually begin sentences, and Row #2 gives pronouns that usually come after the verb. Rows #3 and #4 list pronouns that describe a connection (**my** mother) or ownership (**my** bike).

A.   Write your own sentences using two pronouns each time.

For example: Dana had to give **it** back to **her** sister.

1. A sentence using two of **I, he, me, him**.

_____

2. A sentence using two of **she, he, her, him**.

_____

3. A sentence using two of **you, they, it, us**.

_____

4. A sentence using two of **we, it, your, their**.

_____

5. A sentence using two of **hers, I, them, our**.

_____

6. A sentence using two of **my, theirs, mine, you**.

_____

Name: _____

**Lesson 16 — Commas for Times
            and Dates**

Date: _____

A time or a date is made up of different parts:

The time of day:	8:00 p.m.
The name of the day:	Friday
Name of the month and date number:	October 31 <small>(sometimes you don't need the number)</small>
The year:	2001

You can use all of these parts when you describe a date, or you can use just one or two of them. Always follow the order that you see above — time, day, month, year. When you use a date in your sentences, **always put a comma between each part**.

For example: Franco is having a party that starts at 8:00 p.m., Friday, October 31, 2001.

A.   Put commas where they belong.

1. Independence Day comes on Tuesday July 4 this year.

2. What were you doing on Wednesday December 30?

3. George Washington was born on February 22 1732.

4. John F. Kennedy Senior died at 12:01 p.m. November 22 1963.

5. My computer shows the date as Saturday January 1 1900.

6. My calendar shows the date as Saturday January 1 2000.

7. Jay's parents were married on Tuesday August 26 1979.

8. There is going to be a school assembly at 9:30 a.m. Friday June 2.

9. The first day humans walked on the moon was July 20 1969.

10. The last time my family and I went on a vacation was in July 1999.

Can you remember the best day of your life? Fill in the following sentence, and put commas in the right places.

_____ _____ _____ was the best day of my life!
<small>(day of the week)</small>   <small>(month & date number)</small>   <small>(year)</small>

— p.m. means "12:01 at noon until 12:00 midnight."
— a.m. means "12:01 in the morning until 12:00 noon."

UNIT TWO   Name: _____

Lesson 17 — Commas and Addresses   Date: _____

When you use an address in a sentence, you may use all these different parts:

The apartment or unit number:	Apt. 82 {or Unit 61}
The street number (two parts):	1123 Bartman Street
Name of the city:	North Park
Name of the state or province:	Colorado
Country:	United States

You can use all of these parts when you describe an address, or you can use just one or two of them. Always follow the order that you see above — apartment or unit number (if necessary), street number, city, state or province, country. In sentences, always put a comma between each part.

A.   Put commas where they belong.

1. My older sister goes to university in Lincoln Nebraska.

2. Marie used to live in Versailles France.

3. Eric's mom just landed a job in Calgary Alberta Canada.

4. Have you ever been to Disneyworld Orlando Florida?

5. Satish is moving to 24 Goldfish Crescent Nome Alaska.

6. The best restaurant in Texas is The Steakhouse 212 Norton Street Laredo.

7. Do you know anyone from Vancouver Canada?

8. Natasha's best friend lives in Apartment 32B 59 Jefferson Avenue.

9. My uncle lives in Unit 10-D 46 Appletree Lane Butte Montana.

10. The President's brother lives at 22 Delaware Street Washington D.C.

E. JOHNSON
15 DASERIE RD.
THOROLD, ONT.
NZ-6J2

Now, write down **your** full address in a sentence. Be sure to include the number of your apartment or house and the names of your street, city, and state or province. Add the zip code or postal code if you can remember it. Don't forget the commas!

I live at _____

Name: _____

Lesson 18 — Commas

Date: _____

Commas are needed to separate three or more items in a series.*

For example:
The four seasons are Spring, Summer, Autumn, and Winter.
"Early to bed and early to rise makes someone healthy, wealthy, and wise."

A.   Put commas where they are needed.

1. This blanket is big fluffy and warm.

2. Billy-Bob Bubba-Joe and Buddy-Boy are the names of my brothers.

3. Professional ballerinas must be graceful agile and flexible.

4. Professional football players must be strong tough and fast.

5. School teaches much more than Reading Writing and Arithmetic.

6. My mother's hair is long thick and brown.

7. Phil's three favorite teams are the Blue Jays the Cowboys and the Lakers.

8. We won't be in town on the Thursday Friday and Saturday of next week.

B.   Make your own sentences.
     Name 3 or 4 things that you **own**.

For example: I own a coat, a boat, a hat, and a cat.

1. _____.

     Now name 3 or 4 words that **describe** you.

For example: I am little, smart, fast, and tough.

2. _____.

*Note to teachers: it is also entirely acceptable to omit the final comma in the list.

Name: _____

Lesson 19 — The Grammar Games!   Date: _____

A.   Draw a picture of Foo-Foo the poodle shouting: "Bark bark bark? Bark bark bark?"
Beside him is an empty bowl. The cupboard is empty. The Dog Chow box is in the
garbage can.

Is Foo-Foo asking questions? What is he trying to say? Make two guesses.

1. _____

2. _____

B.   Look at the three lists of nouns below (the same lists from Lesson 14).

Now — make a giant sentence, using as many words from the three lists as you can.
If you can make one giant sentence using ALL OF THE NOUNS on ALL THREE LISTS,
you're a champion! Remember to use commas to separate three or more items in a series.

Persons: Kareem, Jody, Kevin, Lisa, Maria, mother, father, people, student....
Places: New York, Seattle, California, park, school, mall, record store....
Things: jeans, dog, wallet, watch, skateboard, roller blades, purse, earrings....

_____

_____

_____

_____

_____

_____

Name: _____

Lesson 20 — Review   Date: _____

A.   Write "Fair!" beside the questions that are whole sentences, and write "Foul!" beside the questions that are not whole sentences. Also, underline all the nouns (the words that name people, places, and things.

Example. _Fair!_   Does **Tyra** like to play **baseball**?

_____   1. Does Jason like to play football?

_____   2. Is Pokémon a?

_____   3. Did Margarita visit Grampa at the senior citizens' home?

_____   4. Does Rashida love music?

_____   5. Will Tyrone's hit land inside the?

_____   6. A new screen-saver for your computer?

B.   Take one line from the above list that is not a whole question. Now, fix it by adding words to the beginning or to the end.

1. _____

C.   Finish the following sentences with a list of **three** (or more) people, places, and things. Remember to use commas!

1. I am friends with _____

_____ .

2. Some places I like to visit are _____

_____ .

3. I would like to buy _____

_____ .

D.   Write one long sentence inviting people to a party at your place. Give the exact time and the exact address. Remember to put in commas where they belong.

_____

_____ .

Name: _____

Lesson 21 — Nouns and Numbers.
      Single and Plural

Date: _____

A **noun** is a word that names a **person**, **place**, or **thing**.
A **singular noun** is a word that names **one** person, place, or thing.
Plural nouns are words that name **two or more** persons, places, or things.

A. Usually, all you have to do is add an **s** to turn a singular noun into a plural noun.

1. airplane___      4. book___      7. friend___

2. cat___   5. sister___   8. donut___

3. cake___   6. game___   9. mall___

As a class, think of six more nouns that need an **s** to become plural:

1. _____   3. _____   5. _____

2. _____   4. _____   6. _____

B. For singular nouns that end in **s**, **ss**, **sh**, **ch**, **x**, and **z**, add **es** to make them plural.

1. bus_____      4. dress_____      7. box_____

2. pass_____   5. batch_____   8. fax_____

3. dish_____   6. church_____   9. buzz_____

As a class, think of three more:

1. _____   2. _____   3. _____

C. Next, there is a small list of "rebel" singular nouns that follow a completely different rule. To make them plural, you have to change the spelling. Do you know the plural form for any of these nouns? Your teacher will ask you to spell it out loud, so the rest of you can copy it.

1. man >> _____men_____   4. candy >> _____   7. tooth >> _____

2. woman >> _____   5. half >> _____   8. goose >> _____

3. mouse >> _____   6. foot >> _____   9. child >> _____

D. Finally, there are a few nouns that don't change their spelling at all.

     Fish, **moose**, and **sheep** are three examples.

There is one dish, and two dishes, but one fish and **two fish**, although some little kids say "fishies".
One peep, and two peeps, but one sheep, two sheep, or a **thousand sheep**!
One goose, two geese; one papoose, two papooses; but **not** two *meese* or *moose*s! Just moose!

21

Name: _____

Lesson 22 — Singular Nouns and Ownership

Date: _____

Apostrophes (pronounced, "a-PAW-stra-fees").

A **noun** is a word that names a **person**, **place**, or **thing**.
A **singular noun** is a word that names one person, place, or thing.
To make a singular noun show **possession**, **ownership**, or **relationship**,
     add an **apostrophe** and an s.

Jimmy >> Jimmy**'s**   Jimmy's skateboard lost a wheel.   (ownership)
                          Jimmy's arm is broken.
                          Jimmy's mother is upset.   (relationship)

boy >> boy**'s**   That boy's brother is my friend.
girl >> girl**'s**   That poor girl's computer caught a bad virus.
church >> church**'s**   Only my church's bells were ringing.

A.   Change the singular nouns to show ownership by adding **'s.**

1. child_____   7. supermodel_____   13. flower____

2. toy_____   8. sandal_____   14. doctor_____

3. house_____   9. goose_____   15. teddy bear____

4. cookie_____   10. father_____   16. knee____

5. woman____   11. foot_____   17. girl____

6. guy_____   12. neighbor_____   18. teacher____

B.   Take four of the singular possessive nouns above, and make sentences out of them.
      For fun, try to use a second noun from the list in your sentences.

Examples: The **supermodel's cookie** was crumbly. The **teacher's goose** was in the oven.
               (7)   (4)   (18)   (9)

1. _____.

2. _____.

3. _____.

4. _____.

Name: _____

Lesson 23 — Plural Nouns and   Date: _____
             Ownership

Apostrophes (pronounced, "a-PAW-stra-fees").

A **noun** is a word that names a **person**, **place**, or **thing**.
Plural nouns are words that name **two or more** persons, places, or things.
To make most **plural nouns** show **possession**, **ownership**, or **relationship**,
       add an **apostrophe** *after* the **s**.

boys >> boy**s'**   The boys' all-star team won the championship.
girls >> girl**s'**   The girls' computers all got viruses.
church >> churche**s'**   All the churches' bells were ringing.

Some plural nouns do not end in an **s**.
Examples: men, women, children, sheep.
In these cases, do the same thing that you did for singular nouns —
       add an apostrophe and an s.

men >> men's   The men's basketball team lost last night.
women >> women's   The women's basketball team beat them.
sheep >> sheep's   The sheep's owner looked like one of his sheep.

A.   Change the plural nouns to show ownership by adding an **'** or an **'s**.

1. children____   7. supermodels____   13. flowers____

2. toys____   8. sandals____   14. doctors____

3. houses____   9. geese____   15. teddy bears____

4. cookies____   10. parents____   16. knees____

5. women____   11. feet____   17. girls____

6. boys____   12. neighbors____   18. teachers____

B.   Take four of the plural possessive nouns above and make sentences out of them.

1. _____.

2. _____.

3. _____.

4. _____.

Name: _____

Lesson 24 — Pronouns Showing
Ownership, Relationship

Date: _____

A pronoun is a word used in place of a noun.
There are many kinds of pronouns. These are the ones we use the most.

	SINGULAR					**PLURAL**		
1.	I	you	she	he	it	we	you	they
2.	me	you	her	him	it	us	you	them
3.	my	your	her	his	its	our	your	their
4.	mine	yours	hers	his		ours	yours	theirs

Row 3 lists pronouns that describe a relationship (**his** mother) or ownership (**his** bike). The word **his** replaces a word like **Deion's** or **Mary's**.
Row 4 also lists pronouns that describe a relationship or ownership, but these pronouns are used in a different way. They come after the verb.

Examples: That is **my** bike.   That bike is **mine**.   (NOT, "That is mine bike.")
            That is **her** locker.   That locker is **hers**.   (NOT, "That is hers locker.")

A.   Replace each pair of sentences with two sentences using a pronoun.
         Each pair of sentences says the same thing, but in a different way.

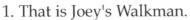

Examples: 1. Those are Tamatha's shoes.   Those shoes are Tamatha's.
               (a) <u>Those are **her** shoes.</u>   (b) <u>Those shoes are **hers**.</u>

1. That is Joey's Walkman.   That Walkman is Joey's.

(a) _____ .   (b) _____ .

2. The party was Halle's idea.   The idea for the party was Halle's.

(a) _____ .   (b) _____ .

B.   Fill in the blanks with the correct pronouns.

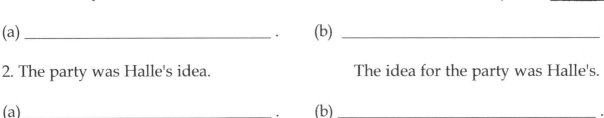

1. That skateboard belongs to you.

(a) That is _____ skateboard.   (b) That skateboard is _____ .

2. That basketball belongs to those guys over there.

(a) That is _____ basketball.   (b) That basketball is _____ .

Name: _____

Lesson 25 — Pronouns Showing   Date: _____
           Ownership, Relationship

A pronoun is a word used in place of a noun. A few pronouns we haven't studied yet are:

someone, somebody	someone's, somebody's
anyone, anybody	anyone's, anybody's,
no one, nobody	no one's, nobody's.

Someone means basically the same thing as **somebody**,
anyone means the same thing as **anybody**,
and **no one** means the same thing as **nobody**.
These pronouns describe people whose names we don't know, or even people who are not there.

A.   Change each sentence by using **someone, somebody, anyone, anybody, no one,** or **nobody.**

Example: I hope <u>a player</u> on our team scores soon.
               >> I hope <u>someone</u> on our team scores soon.

1. <u>A person</u> left her sunglasses in the cloakroom.

>> _____ .

2. <u>Not one student</u> in this room knows my secret identity.

>> _____ .

3. Does <u>a single person</u> on this team know how to pass?

>> _____ ?

B.   Change each sentence by using **someone's, somebody's, anyone's, anybody's, no one's,** or **nobody's.**
               Example: <u>A person's</u> shoes are still in the room.
                            >> <u>Somebody's</u> shoes are still in the room.

1. That's <u>not one person's</u> business but my own.

>> _____ .

2. It's a tough job, but <u>a person's</u> got to do it.

>> _____ .

3. Harvey can hack into <u>any person's</u> computer.

>> _____ .

Name: _____

Lesson 26 — Nouns and Pronouns   Date: _____

A.   Read the following paragraph. A blank space follows every noun that should be
       replaced by a pronoun from the list below. Put the correct pronoun into each blank.

PRONOUNS to use: they, no one's/nobody's, them, you, him, your, their, it, my

One summer, Billy and Annika made an obstacle course in (Billy and Annika's) _____

yard. (Billy and Annika) _____ invited all (Billy and Annika's) _____ friends

to come over and play with (Billy and Annika) _____. First (the kids) _____

all jumped over a lawn chair. Next, (the kids) _____ ran through a maze drawn with

chalk on the driveway. (The kids') _____ last challenge was to throw a basketball

through the net without it touching the rim. (Not one of the kids') _____ shot

made it in smoothly except for Billy's.

      "A perfect swish! I'm the winner!" Billy rejoiced. "What's (Billy's — he is talking about

himself) _____ prize?"

      "Well, what would (Billy) _____ like?" the other kids asked.

      "I want all of (the other kids') _____ candy!"

      "We're not going to give you *ALL* of (the candy) _____ !"

      "Why don't we give (Billy) _____ half of our candy," Annika suggested to the
others. "Then let's play again."

B. Write the correct pronoun from the list below into each blank in the following paragraph.

PRONOUNS to use: it, someone/somebody, mine, you, my, her

"Thank _____ for coming to _____ birthday party," Tammy said to _____ guests. "I

hope _____ brought a cake because _____ little brother just knocked [**my** cake]

_____ off the table, and ____ fell onto the carpet."

Name: _____

Lesson 27 — Capital Letters: Date: _____
   Movie Titles, Book Titles, Story Titles

Begin the first word and all important words in the titles of movies and books with a capital letter. Do not use capital letters for words such as **the, a, an, of, in, by, and, for, at, to, under, with** — unless one of them is the first word in the title.

For example: **Snow White and the Seven Dwarfs**

A.   Rewrite the following movie titles using capital letters.

the wizard of oz _____

batman returns _____

how the grinch stole christmas _____

star wars: return of the jedi _____

B.   Now, write down the names of four of your favorite movies:

1. _____
2. _____
3. _____
4. _____

C.   Rewrite the following book titles using capital letters.

Example: **Charlie and the Chocolate Factory**

anne of green gables _____

wonderbaby and the flying bathroom _____

the wind in the willows _____

the magic schoolbus _____

pippi longstocking _____

D.   Now, write down the names of four of your favorite books:

1. _____
2. _____
3. _____
4. _____

Name: _____

Lesson 28 — Commas

Date: _____

Use a comma to set off the name of a person when you name that person directly in a sentence. Sometimes a comma has to be used before and after the name.

"Jennifer, when did you decide to become a scientist?"
"When did you decide to become a scientist, Jennifer?"
"When did you decide, Jennifer, to become a scientist?"

We also need to put commas after the words **Oh**, **Well**, **Yes**, and **No** when they are the first words in a sentence.

"Oh, I can't remember."   "Well, that's a long story."
"Yes, I would like a swimming pool filled with bubbles."   "No, I don't think so."

A. Put the comma where it belongs in the following sentences.

1. Freddy do you know where I put my pen?

2. Well did you look behind your chair?

3. Yes and it isn't there.

4. I'll bet you tucked it behind your ear again Sally and then forgot about it.

5. No I don't think I did that this time.

6. Well maybe you should check.

7. Fine Freddy I will.

8. Oh there it is!

9. Thank you Freddy.

10. You're welcome Sally.

B.   Think of something that you would like someone in this class to do. It can be funny or serious. Now, write the sentence in the space below.

Example: Tony, could you please give our teacher a detention?

1. _____

Name: _____

Lesson 29 — Revenge of The Grammar Games!

Date: _____

Make funny sentences using the lists below.

For example, The _____ _____ _____ _____ _____.
         NOUN (Person)   VERB   PRONOUN   ADJECTIVE   NOUN (Thing)

Could become: The ___girl___ chewed _her_ _smelly_ _toes___.

Or: The detective kicked __his__ __hairy__ _computer_.

Feel free to add your own adjectives, nouns, pronouns and verbs to these lists!

ADJECTIVES	NOUNS		PRONOUNS	VERBS
	PERSONS	**THINGS**		
yummy	girl	toes	her	chew
smelly	boy	shoe	hers	drink
pretty	angel	heart	his	marry
silly	soldier	leg	him	buy
hairy	mother	phone	it	pull
sticky	alien	spaceship	its	kick
strange	detective	lollipop		lick
small	fairy	computer		push
cute	princess	tutu		tickle
gross	father	pumpkin		annoy
weird	president	ankle		watch
cool	teacher	television		kiss

1. You _____ the _____ _____.
        VERB   *ADJECTIVE*   *NOUN*

2. The _____ has a _____ _____.
      NOUN   *ADJECTIVE*   *NOUN (Thing.)*

3. I want to _____ that _____ _____.
           VERB   *ADJECTIVE*   *NOUN*

4. That _____ is so _____, I'd like to _____ _____.
       NOUN   *ADJECTIVE*   *VERB*   *PRONOUN*

5. Once upon a time there was a _____ who wanted to _____ all
                                 NOUN (Person)   *VERB*

of the _____ _____ in the kingdom.
       ADJECTIVE   *NOUN (Thing)*

6. I know a _____ who would like _____ _____ to be _____.
           NOUN (Person)   *PRONOUN* *NOUN (Thing)*   *ADJECTIVE*

Name: _____

Lesson 30 — Review

Date: _____

A.   Some of the nouns in these sentences need to be turned into plurals, and some of the nouns need to have an **'s** or an **s'** added to them to show possession or relationship. Write the corrected sentence under the one with mistakes.

Example: My mother sister owns ten cat .

My mother**'s** sister owns ten cat**s**.

1. Jimmy team won two trophy in the last tournament.

_____

2. Both of my older sister own dog .

_____

3. The children favorite movie are "Lion King" and "101 Dalmations".

_____

4. All of his friend bike have bell that ring loudly.

_____

B.   Replace each pair of sentences with two sentences using a pronoun.
Each pair of sentences says the same thing, but in a different way.

Examples: 1. That is Timmy's Walkman.   That Walkman is Timmy's.
   (a) That is **his** Walkman.   (b) That Walkman is **his**.

1. Those are Amy's books.   Those books are Amy's.

(a) _____ .   (b) _____ .

2. Playing Sega was those guys' idea.   The idea to play Sega was all those guys'.

(a) _____ .   (b) _____ .

C.   Fill in the blanks with the correct pronouns.

1. That frisbee belongs to you.

(a) That is _____ frisbee.   (b) That frisbee is _____ .

2. "The world belongs to us, Igor!"

(a) "This is _____ world, Igor!"   (b) "The world is _____ , Igor!"

Name: _____

Lesson 31 — Verbs   Date: _____

(a) A verb usually shows action. It shows what someone or something **does**.
(b) A verb can also show what someone or something **is**.
(c) A verb can also show what someone or something **has**.

Some verbs showing action: **buy, fight, run, play, eat, comb, sing, act, laugh**.

Some verbs showing what someone or something is: **am, are, is, equals, looks like**.

Some verbs showing what someone or something has: **has, have, own, possess**.

The verb part of a sentence can be one word.
It can also be two or more words, and is usually called a verb phrase.

One word.   Jackie **likes** ice cream. She **is** very happy.
                   Tawanda **played** Nintendo for two hours.

Two words: Jackie **is eating** some ice cream right now.
("verb phrase")   Tawanda **was playing** Nintendo at 9 o'clock last night.
                   Buster **will have** his new Macintosh by tomorrow night.

A.   Draw lines under the verbs in the following sentences.

1. Mateo knows me better than anyone else.

2. Cecily is Harvey's youngest sister.

3. I am eating a peanut butter and jelly sandwich.

4. Samantha looks very pretty in her new outfit.

5. Bert was talking during class.

6. Bruce learned a new language during his trip to China.

7. Eduardo is planning a surprise party for his father's 40th birthday.

B.   Make up your own sentences using two-word verb phrases
        Example: I **am thinking** about my new puppy.

1. (Use "was eating") _____ .

2. (Use "is playing") _____ .

3. (Use "will see") _____ .

Name: _____

Lesson 32 — Verbs

Date: _____

The verb part of a sentence can be one word.
It can also be two or more words, and is usually called a **verb phrase**.

Two words: Jackie **has eaten** lots of ice cream in her life.
Mr. Jones **had been** a pilot for two years (before he became a teacher).

Three words: Tawanda **has been surfing** the Internet since she was seven.
Maria **had been working** at two jobs before she caught a flu.
Buster **will be testing** his new Macintosh tomorrow night.

A.   Identify the verb phrases by underlining them.

1. We will be swimming in the neighbor's pool at around four o'clock.

2. Suzie has been preparing food for the picnic all morning.

3. Jesse has been bungee-jumping for a couple of years.

4. Mark will travel to Africa next year.

5. The Thompson twins have been spying on us all summer.

6. Danielle has downloaded three games from the Internet in the last week.

B.   Make up sentences using the two-word and three-word verb phrases below.

1. will find	3. had seen	5. had been sitting
2. have been trying	4. will be leaving	6. has skipped

1. _____.

2. _____.

3. _____.

4. _____.

5. _____.

6. _____.

Lesson 33 — Adjectives

An adjective is a word that describes a noun or pronoun.
Adjectives can describe size, weight, age, color, motion, beauty, intelligence and many other qualities.

big, small, heavy, light, black, red, spotted, speedy, slow, American, beautiful, smart.

Adjectives can be used in different parts of a sentence.

My cat is **big**.
My **big** cat's name is Bigglesworth.
Big Bigglesworth likes to eat **big** bowls of cat chow!

A.   Draw a line under each adjective in the sentences below.

For example: The <u>new</u> girl seems <u>shy</u>.

1. Eli's blue backpack is heavy.

2. The donuts in the cafeteria are yucky.

3. Janine's brother is cute!

4. Tomorrow is supposed to be breezy, sunny, and warm.

5. Spotted leopards can be seen in beautiful Africa.

6. Téa hopes to buy a short, plaid, green and red kilt.

7. Dolphins are intelligent.

8. Serena's dad is a tall, quick, and excellent basketball player.

9. Justine's Canadian cousin is a wild and crazy dancer.

B. For the following sentences, rearrange the adjectives from each jumbled group in front of the noun. Compare your list to those of other students. Whose list sounds just right?

Example.   Look at the *(white, little, pretty)* flower.
Look at the **pretty, little, white** flower.

1. Aviva's new kitten is *(furry, soft, cuddly, cute)*_____ and _____.

2. My cousin lives in a *(orange, small, ugly)* _____ house.

Name: _____

Lesson 34 — Verbs and Adjectives

Date: _____

A verb is a word that shows **action**, **being**, and **having**.
An adjective is a word that **describes** a noun or a pronoun.

A. Find the **verbs** and **adjectives** in the following sentences.
Draw a circle around each verb. Draw a line under each adjective.

1. Keisha dances in shiny, red shoes.

2. Jorge has curly, black hair.

3. Apples are sweet and crunchy.

4. Kelsey is kind as well as pretty.

5. Amelia always wears her soft, blue dress to church.

6. In Autumn, the leaves change to red and yellow before they fall from the trees.

7. This morning, Bob combed his clean, tangled hair and washed his dirty face.

8. At breakfast, he poured cold juice into his porridge and warm milk into his cup.

9. He watered his dry lawn and fed his hungry dog.

10. As Bob tripped over Fluffy the cat, he wished he had never left the safety of his soft, cozy bed.

B. Now, look around the room. Describe five things. Underline the adjectives you use to describe what you see, and circle the verbs.

For example: There (is) a tall, blond kid in front of me.

1. _____.

2. _____.

3. _____.

4. _____.

5. _____.

Name: _____

**Lesson 35 — Adverbs: Describing
When, Where, How**

Date: _____

An adjective is a word that describes a noun or a pronoun. Adjectives describe size, weight, age, color, motion, beauty, intelligence and many other qualities.

Other words, called **adverbs**, are also used to describe things.
Adverbs describe the **time** when something happens, the **place** where something happens, **how** something happens, and **why** something happens.
First, let's look at words that answer **when**, **where**, and **how**.

When >>   yesterday, today, tomorrow, now, later. . .
Where >>   here, there, east, west, north, south, backward, forward, home, away. . .
How >>   slowly, quickly, lazily, happily, quietly. . .

Answer the following questions (or commands) with words **from the lists above**. Use whole sentences.

For example: When did you go to the concert?
                    <u>We went to the concert **yesterday**.</u>

1. When will you get a DVD player?

_____.

2. Where do most students go after school?

_____.

3. Describe how a turtle walks.

_____.

4. Describe how a rabbit runs.

_____.

5. When are you going to clean your room?

_____.

6. In which direction is Mexico from the United States border?

_____.

7. In which direction is Canada from the United States border?

_____.

8. How do you do your homework?

_____.

9. Where are you?

_____.

10. Where is your teacher?

_____.

Name: _____

Lesson 36 — Adverb Phrases   Date: _____
   Describing When, Where, How, Why

Adjectives describe nouns and pronouns.
Adverbs describe everything else. The most important jobs for adverbs are to describe
when, where, how, and why something happens. Adverbs can be single words.

When >>   yesterday, today, tomorrow, now, later. . .
Where >>   here, there, east, west, north, south, backward, forward, home, away. . .
How >>   slowly, quickly, lazily, happily, quietly. . .

Adverbs can also be groups of words.

When >>   at 5 o'clock; in a little while; two days ago; next week; right now. . . .
Where >> in my backyard; at the mall; under your chair; in California. . . .
How # 1 *describes how something is happening*
        >>   in a hurry; at a slow pace; in a very lazy way; with a happy smile. . . .
How # 2 *describes how someone travels somewhere*
        >>   by bus; in his mother's car; by plane; by walking. . . .
Why >>   because he wanted to buy some candy; because he wanted to get rich. . . .

A.   Make up a question for each answer.

Examples:
1. Because he wanted to buy a can of pop.   2. At 7 o'clock.
   <u>Why did Terry go to the store?</u>   <u>When did Mariah start the concert?</u>

1. By train.
_____?

2. Next door to me.
_____?

3. Because he likes the color green.
_____?

4. In a hurry.
_____?

5. On foot.
_____?

6. Because we're friends.
_____?

7. A year from now.
_____?

8. Because the turtle kept on walking while the rabbit took a nap.
_____?

Name: _____

Lesson 37 — Contractions

Date: _____

Contractions are two words joined together with a letter or letters left out.
Put an apostrophe { ' } wherever the letters have been left out.
In all of these examples, the letter **o** was taken out and replaced with an apostrophe.

is not	>>	**isn't**		are not	>>	**aren't**
was not	>>	**wasn't**		were not	>>	**weren't**
does not	>>	**doesn't**		do not	>>	**don't**
has not	>>	**hasn't**		have not	>>	**haven't**

had not >> **hadn't**
did not >> **didn't**

A. Fill in the blanks with the right contraction.

1. "Where is your dad? _____ he supposed to pick us up here at 7?"

2. "Just standing here waiting right now _____ very fun."

3. "Maybe he's got a good excuse for being late. We _____ know what has happened."

4. "Yeah, right. Maybe he _____ know what time it is."

5. "No, I mean, what if we _____ waiting in the right place?"

6. "If you want to worry about unlikely things, you had better hope he _____ forgotten how to drive!"

7. "And I really hope he _____ just forget about *us* !"

B. In groups, make up sentences using the list of contractions from above. Choose the four sentences that you like the best, and write them down.

For example: Mallory didn't go to the North Pole yesterday.
　　　　　　Bryan doesn't keep elephants in his fridge.

1. _____.

2. _____.

3. _____.

4. _____.

Contractions are two words joined together with a letter or letters left out.
Put an apostrophe { ' } wherever the letters have been left out.

I am	>>	**I'm**		I have	>>	**I've**
you are	>>	**you're**		you have	>>	**you've**
we are	>>	**we're**		we have	>>	**we've**
they are	>>	**they're**		they have	>>	**they've**

he is, she is, it is	>>	**he's, she's, it's**	
he has, she has, it has	>>	**he's, she's, it's**	*(same contraction)*

A. Fill in the blanks with the right contraction.

My first day at school, the teacher, Ms. Fabrice, called me Mabel.

"Sorry," I said. "_____ not Mabel. _____ the one in the red shirt."

The teacher said, "Oh, then you must be Erica. _____ supposed to be in the next room

with Mr. Mankey. _____ a very good teacher."

Well, I took one look at the students in Mr. Mankey's class and went right back to Ms.

Fabrice's class.

"_____ got to be kidding me," I said to her. "But even if you *are* kidding me,

_____ not very funny. The kids in Mr. Mankey's class are way younger than me, and

_____ even got their mothers with them."

Ms. Fabrice said, "But _____ Erica, right? Erica Van Mueller?"

"No, _____ mistaken. _____ Erica Keeler."

"Oh! _____ sorry, Erica. _____ in the right class, then. I guess _____ both

started the year on the wrong foot. I hope we can ignore this beginning and start fresh."

B. Make up three sentences of your own, using the contractions from the lists at the top
of the page.

For example: No, **I'm** not Batman.
               He's in my kitchen, eating bat food.

1. _____.

2. _____.

3. _____.

4. _____.

Name: _____

Lesson 39 — The Grammar Games!

Date: _____

CROSSWORD PUZZLE

A. Find the verbs in the following sentences, then write them into their corresponding boxes.

Across 6. I ate gummy worms for lunch.

A7. Robert kicked Jamie on the shin.

A9. Delilah is a liar.

Down 4. Francesca paints frescoes.

D5. Amy had a fun day.

D8. Pam earned ten dollars today.

B. Find the adjectives in the following sentences, then write them into their boxes.

A4. Zoe's dress was a peach color.

A13. This closet is dark.

A16. Mr. Meir's house is creepy.

D1 That hill is very steep!

D14. Last week was rainy.

D15. I don't want to eat with a bent spoon!

C. Find the adverbs in the following sentences, then write them into their boxes.

A1. Bart sat silently.

A10. See the polar bears walk north.

A11. "Goodbye," she said tearfully.

D2. I said I'd do it later!

D3. Lola saw him yesterday.

D12. Please step forward.

Name: _____

Date: _____

A.   Verbs and adjectives. Find the **verbs** and **adjectives** in the following sentences. Draw a circle around each verb or verb phrase. Draw a line under each adjective.

1. Jackson always wears his new, gray, suit to church.

2. Manny has straight, black hair, but his sister Amy has curly, red hair.

3. While Bob was washing the dirty dishes, Tommy was looking for a dry towel.

4. Keisha's friend will be dancing in her shiny, pointed, silver shoes.

5. That new computer is fast, light, and colorful.

B.   Adverbs that answer **why, when, where,** and **how.** Make up a question for each answer.

Examples: (a) Because he wanted to buy a new CD.
                         <u>Why did Rufus go to the music store?</u>
                   (b) At 5 o'clock.
                         <u>When does that new cartoon start?</u>

1. In his room.

_____ **?**

2. Because that's her favorite group

_____ **?**

3. By plane

_____ **?**

4. Slowly

_____ **?**

5. Tomorrow

_____ **?**

C. Write these sentences over again, changing each contraction into two separate words.

Example: **You're** my best friend, and **she's** your sister's best friend.
            You are my best friend, and **she is** your sister's best friend.

1.   **I'm** not going to her house tonight, because **she's** in Kansas City.

_____ .

2.   They **haven't** won many games this year; **they've** had a lot of injuries.

_____ .

3.   **We've** got to get there by 7 o'clock, or else they **won't** let us in.

_____ .

Name: _____

Lesson 41 — Exclamations!

Date: _____

Most sentences are groups of words that tell us something.
Other sentences are questions — groups of words that ask us something.

Exclamations show strong feeling, such as excitement, surprise, warning, or anger.
An exclamation can be a word, a group of words or a whole sentence.
Exclamations are always followed by exclamation points.

Excitement:	one word.	Great!
	phrase	What a beautiful day!
	sentence	This sure is a beautiful day!

A. Show the difference between questions, exclamations, and ordinary sentences.
Put a period, a question mark, or an exclamation point at the end of each line.

1. Watch out for that tree

2. I'm falling asleep

3. Heather screamed loudly, "That is so amazing "

4. Why are you bothering me

5. Hey, you — get off of my lawn

6. Where have all the flowers gone

7. They've moved to the United States from Canada

8. The man shouted, "That is incredible "

9. Wow

B. Can you think of three things that show strong feeling? Make three sentences that are exclamations!

1. _____!

2. _____!

3. _____!

Name: _____

Lesson 42 — Paragraphs and Capital Letters

Date: _____

We usually use sentences when we talk or write to each other. When we speak or write a lot of sentences in a row, we try to group our sentences into **paragraphs**.

A paragraph is a group of sentences about one topic.

A.   Read the following paragraph.

Dear Kelly:

Can you believe that it's already been a week since we left Camp Linguino?! It feels like we were there only yesterday. Do you remember the time our group hiked out to Lake Parleton? I didn't think it was possible for water to be so cold in the middle of summer! There was a good part, though — when you stepped on that frog in your bare feet and jumped about a mile into the air screaming your head off! I never laughed so hard before in my life! Then when we had lunch you found three fat bugs stuck in the mayonnaise in your sandwich! That whole trip was so funny. I'm definitely going back next year. I hope you'll be there, too!

Your friend,

Jennifer Schadenfreude

P.S. I hope that rash you got from the poison ivy is clearing up!

B.   The next paragraph is written well, but the writer forgot to use capital letters!
Draw a circle around each word that should be a capital.

dear jennifer:

thank you for your letter. the rash is getting better but it's still very itchy and the mosquito bites make it worse. unfortunately, i don't remember that trip to lake parleton as clearly as you do. i remember the cold water, the frog, the bugs in my sandwich, and the walk our group went on through the valley after lunch. however, everything got kind of blurry after i got hit on the head by a falling rock. please write to me again and tell me about everything that happened after my accident. i hope we had fun — but even if we did, i don't think i'll be coming back to camp linguino. it seems to bring me bad luck.

your friend,

kelly blackett

Name: _____

Lesson 43 — Writing Paragraphs

Date: _____

A paragraph is a group of sentences about one topic.

A. Read the following paragraph.

    My best friend Fredrika and I have lived on the same street for our whole lives. She was my first friend outside of my own family. I met her when I was only two years old. We've changed a lot since then, but our friendship is the same, and I hope it never changes. Fredrika is pretty, smart, and fun to be with. I feel lucky that we're friends.

B. Now, write your own paragraph. Write about a friend of yours, and explain why you like to be around him or her. Or, write about your mother, father, grandparents, or other family members. Describe their good qualities. Then, after school, show your paragraph to that person.

_____

_____

_____

_____

_____

_____

_____

_____

_____

_____

Name: _____

Lesson 44 — Writing Paragraphs   Date: _____

A.   Write your own short paragraph about a trip to the beach, or a trip to the mall, or a trip to visit a friend. There should be at least **five sentences** in your paragraph, but you can write even more sentences. Just make sure that all your sentences are on the same topic.

_____

_____

_____

_____

_____

_____

B.   Now, your teacher will mark the parts that need to be changed. Write down the new version in the space below, using the corrections your teacher has suggested.

_____

_____

_____

_____

_____

_____

Lesson 45 — Usage: I / me   Date: _____

The word **I** usually comes at the beginning of sentences, when you tell someone about what you did or what you are doing.

The word **me** usually comes later, when you tell what someone else did to you or for you. You never start a sentence with me.

Wrong >> **Me** am going to a movie tonight.
Right   >> **I** am going to a movie tonight.

Wrong >> My mother helped **I** with my homework.
Right   >> My mother helped **me** with my homework.

If you add another person to each sentence, put **I** and **me** after the other person's name.

Very Wrong! >>   **Me and Joey** are going to a movie tonight.
Wrong >>   **I and Joey** are going to a movie tonight.
Right, Good! >> **Joey and I** are going to a movie tonight.

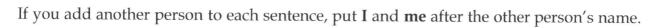

Very Wrong! >>   My mother helped **I and Gloria** with our homework.
Wrong >>   My mother helped **me and Gloria** with our homework.
Right, Good! >> My mother helped **Gloria and me** with our homework.

Fill in each blank with either I or me.

1. Alexis and _____ have tickets to the Quacktreat Toys concert!

2. Grandpa took Danny and _____ to SeaWorld last weekend.

3. Trini and _____ never get to use the remote control when Dad's in the room.

4. Cindy and _____ went to have our pictures taken together.

5. Mrs. Horvath taught Reuben and _____ in the first grade.

6. Do you want to come to the arcade with Pete and _____?

7. Harry and _____ share the same birthday.

8. Mr. Palmer gave Adam and _____ five dollars each to mow his lawn.

9. Suzie and _____ were at camp in July.

Name: _____

Lesson 46 — Quotations

Date: _____

Someone speaks out loud. You hear that person, and write her exact words on a piece of paper.

Harriet asked, "Are we lost in these dark woods?"

That is called a direct quotation. To show those are Harriet's exact words, you put quotation marks at the beginning and the end of her sentence.

You can also tell what Harriet said without using her exact words.

Harriet asked if we were lost in the dark woods.

That is called an indirect quotation. You do not need to use quotation marks.

Write **D.Q.** before each sentence that contains a **direct quotation**.
Write **I.Q.** before each sentence that contains an **indirect quotation**.

_____ 1. "Can I come in? What are you doing in there?" asked Tammy's younger brother, Johnny.

_____ 2. "Don't tell him we're watching TV," Tammy whispered to her friend, Jocelyn.

_____ 3. Jocelyn wanted to know why not.

_____ 4. Tammy explained that she wasn't allowed to watch television after 9:00 p.m.

_____ 5. "If my brother tells on us, we'll be in big trouble," she added.

_____ 6. "Go away!" the two girls yelled. "Leave us alone!"

_____ 7. "You're mean!" said Johnny, and left.

_____ 8. His mother noticed that he looked sad, and asked him what had happened.

_____ 9. Once Johnny had finished telling her, she said she would go talk to the girls about their behavior.

_____ 10. When she opened the door to Tammy's room and saw that the television was on, she said: "Tammy, you're grounded!"

Name: _____

Lesson 47 — Quotations

Date: _____

(a)   Quotation marks always come in pairs.
      One comes at the beginning of a direct quotation, and the other comes at the end.

(b)   A **direct quotation** contains the speaker's exact words.
      Notice the periods, commas, question marks and exclamation points in the following
      direct quotations. You must put them **inside** the quotation marks.

(c)   The first letter in most quotations is a capital.

      "I need a new pair of roller blades," said Marco.
      Whitney shouted, "This is the best pizza I've ever had!"
      "Do you want to go bungee jumping?" asked David.
      David said, "Bungee jumping is a lot of fun."

A.   There is a direct quotation in **all** the sentences below. In each sentence, put the
        quotation marks at the beginning and end of each direct quotation.

1.   Monica wanted to know, Does Charlie like to skateboard?

2.   Mom, can we get a DVD player for Christmas? asked Mimi.

3.   I want to be a famous chef when I grow up, Dee Lishus informed her teacher.

4.   Wally waved his arms, shouting, Hey guys, we're over here!

5.   There will be a test next Thursday, Ms Allamaine informed her class.

6.   Mr. Fuston asked worriedly, How did you get that cut on your foot?

7.   I'm going to try out for the soccer team this year, Justin told his father.

8.   Here's a list of all the CDs I want for my birthday, Jessica said.

9.   Darla looked at the ground, shuffled her feet, and said, I'm sorry.

10. Carlos gave Andy three of his video games, saying: I never play with them any more,
     so you can have them.

Name: _____

Lesson 48 — Quotations

Date: _____

Pretend you are a television reporter. Ask five people in the classroom what their opinion is about lunch time. Do they like their lunches? What is their favorite lunch? Would they like to trade their lunches with someone else? Do they have enough time for lunch?

First, write down their first names.
Next, write a verb that describes their speech (said? complained? shouted?).
Next, write down their exact words in the spaces below.
Finally, write a sentence using the direct quotation.

Example:
Name: **Jeremy**   Verb: **shouted**
Quotation (exact words): "I think lunch time is the best time of the day!"
Sentence: Jeremy shouted loudly, "I think lunch time is the best time of the day!"

1.   Name: _____   Verb: _____

Quotation: "_____."

Sentence: _____.

2.   Name: _____   Verb: _____

Quotation: "_____."

Sentence: _____.

3.   Name: _____   Verb: _____

Quotation: "_____."

Sentence: _____.

4.   Name: _____   Verb: _____

Quotation: "_____."

Sentence: _____.

5.   Name: _____   Verb: _____

Quotation: "_____."

Name: _____

Lesson 49 — The Grammar Games!   Date: _____

A.   Pass the Message, Part One.

1. Think of a favorite TV actress, or of a favorite movie actress. Then write down something that she actually did say or something that she might say. Use quotation marks properly.

   Example: Jena Elfman said, "Greg — you're such a square."

2. Next, form a circle with other members of your class. Each student gets a turn. Whisper your sentence into the ear of the student beside you. This student will pass the message to the next student, until you go all around the circle. The last student to get the message will write it on the board. Then, you will write the original sentence underneath it.

_____.

B.   Pass the Message, Part Two.

1. Think of a favorite TV actor, or of a favorite movie actor. Then write down something that he actually did say or something that he might say. Use quotation marks properly.

   Example: Leonard di Caprio shouted, "I'm the king of the world!"

2. Next, form a circle with other members of your class. Each student gets a turn. Whisper your sentence into the ear of the student beside you. This student will pass the message to the next student, until you go all around the circle. The last student to get the message will write it on the board. Then, you will write the original sentence underneath it.

_____.

C.   Write a letter or an e-mail to a star.   Make use of the Internet.

1. Teacher — make this a real exercise. If you plan to write real letters, supply envelopes, or make them. Ask the students to bring in stamps. If you plan to write e-mails, be sure to include the school's or the classroom's e-mail address so that the stars have a chance to write back to each student.

2. Use the Internet to locate the publicity agencies for each star or for their shows, groups, or teams. These agencies will give you addresses that accept fan mail.

3. All students will write a letter to their favorite actor or music star or sports star. Tell him or her about the three things that you like about them. You may use exclamation points for all three things. Make two copies: send one, and keep the other for display.

4. How long will you have to wait? Who will get the first reply letter?

5. Teacher — make a display of the original letters, and then add each reply as it comes in.

Name: _____

Date: _____

A. Change the **indirect quotations** to **direct quotations**.

Example: Mary said that she liked her pizza with pieces of pineapple.   (indirect)
           Mary said, "I like my pizza with pieces of pineapple."   (direct)

1. Carlos said that he has to go to his mother's house every Saturday for lunch.

_____

2. Gilbert shouted that he was going to buy a new skateboard tomorrow.

_____

3. Consuela complained that she had to do too much homework last week.

_____

B. Change the **direct quotations** to **indirect quotations**.

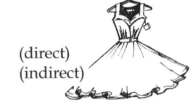

Example: Reuben said, "I like green pepper on my pizza."   (direct)
           Reuben said that he likes green pepper on his pizza.   (indirect)

1. Chita thought, "I'm going to buy myself a new dress."

_____

2. Jim-Bob said, "We have to try a lot harder if we want to win!"

_____

3. Every day, Tara complains, "The wheels on my roller blades wear down too fast."

_____

C. The following sentences use **I** and **me** in the wrong places. Correct each sentence.

Example: **Me and Billy** were talking to the teacher.   (wrong!)
           Billy and I were talking to the teacher.   (right!)

1. Jorge's mother scolded I and Billy for playing soccer near her flowers.

_____

2. Me and Moesha saw a great movie last night!

_____

3. Frankie and me went to the video store, but the owner told I and Frankie to get out!

_____

Name: _____

Lesson 51 — Using **there** at the
beginning of sentences

Date: _____

The word **there** can be used to start a sentence.
Use it when you want to say something in a different way.

Examples: A huge engine is in that truck.
There is a huge engine in that truck.

Is a cell phone on the counter?
Is **there** a cell phone on the counter?

A.   Change the following sentences by using **There** at the beginning.

1. A new quarterback is on our football team.

_____

2. A strange light was in the sky last night.

_____

3. Too many vegetables are on my plate.

_____

4. A lot of great shows were on TV last weekend.

_____

5. A really bad show is on TV tonight.

_____

When you are talking about one person or one thing, start your sentences with "There **is**..."
or "There **was**...." When you are talking about more than one person or thing, start your
sentences with "There **are**..." or "There **were**...."

B.   Fill in the blanks with **is, was, are,** or **were.**

1. There _____ a lot of tornadoes in Texas last year.

2. _____ there much damage caused by last year's tornadoes?

3. Yes, last year there _____ a great deal of damage to homes and farms.

4. I suppose there _____ quite a few people hurt, too.

5. That's true. There_____ five people still in the hospital.

6. _____ there anything we can do to protect ourselves from tornadoes?

7. There _____ several things you can do. Listen to warnings, and find a safe place.

Lesson 52 — Using may and can

Many people use the word **can** when they are asking for permission. They say,

"Can I go to the bathroom?"   or   "Can I have a box of popcorn?"

There is a **better way** to ask for permission. Use the word **may** instead.

"May I go to the bathroom?"   or   "May I have a box of popcorn?"

Try to use the word **may** when you are **asking for permission**.
Try to use the word **can** only when you are talking about **being able to do something**.

Examples: Can Latifah program her laptop to make funny noises?
            Yes, she can do many amazing things.

A.   Fill in the blanks with **may** or **can**.

1. Mom, _____ we go outside soon?

2. Yes, children, you _____ go outside as soon as you finish the dishes.

3. How many students _____ fit inside a sports car?

4. Keisha _____ run the forty yard dash in six seconds.

5. _____ you spell Mississippi?

6. Dad, _____ we watch TV all day long today?

7. No, you certainly _____ not!

8. "_____ your dog do any tricks?" we asked Vernon.

9. "My dog Rover _____ roll right over three times in a row," Vernon said.

10. "Teacher, _____ we play a game when this grammar drill is over?"

Teacher: Try playing a game called "Teacher, may I...?" Choose three or four students at a time. Start them at the back of their rows. In turn, give instructions such as, "Alex, you **may** take so many giant steps, or so many baby steps." To be allowed to take these steps, the student must reply with a full question: "Teacher, may I take two giant steps?"

UNIT SIX

Name: _____

Lesson 53 — Using sit and set

Date: _____

Many people use the verb **set** instead of **sit** to mean sitting or resting or staying in one spot.

Grandma said, "I think I'll just **set** here for a little while."

It is better to use the verb **sit** to mean sitting or resting.
It is better to use the word **set** when you are talking about placing an object somewhere, or putting it down.

		Past	Present
SIT	I	sat, was sitting	sit, am sitting
	he, she, it	sat, was sitting	sits, is sitting
	you, they	sat, were sitting	sit, are sitting
SET	I	set, was setting	set, am setting
	he, she, it	set, was setting	sets, is setting
	you, they	set, were setting	set, are setting

Notice that **sit** changes to **sat** in the past tense, but **set** is the same in past and present.

Example: I **sit** in this chair most of the time, but yesterday I **sat** in the teacher's chair.
I **set** the table most of the time, but yesterday my little brother **set** the table.

A. Fill in the blanks with the correct form of **sit** or **set**.

1. How do you _____ the table?

2. First, you _____ the plates down.

3. Then you _____ the knives, forks, and spoons beside the plates.

4. Finally, the people _____ in their chairs and start eating.

5. Jack said, "I'll just _____ in the car while you get the groceries."

6. The coach said, "_____ down, kids. I have great news."

7. "The president of the league just _____ the schedule for our tournament, and we're going to play the Tigers first!"

8. Marvin was _____ on a dock in the bay, watching the tide come in.

Fun exercise. One student will sit somewhere, or pick something up and set it down. Other students in the class have to describe what the student is doing in a full sentence.

53

Name: _____

**Lesson 54 — Gonna, Gotta, Wanna,
　　　　Hafta, Hasta, Hadda**
　　　　　(not good)

Date: _____

People all over North America take short cuts when they speak English.

Instead of saying **"going to"**, they say **"gonna"**.

Instead of **"got to"**, they say **"gotta"**.　　Instead of **"want to"**, they say **"wanna"**.

Instead of **"have to"**, **"has to"**, and **"had to"** they say **"hafta"**, **"hasta"**, and **"hadda"**.

These short cuts are called "slang". There are times when it is not bad to use slang, but there are more times when you should use proper, formal English, especially when you are writing it.

A.　　Write the following sentences over again, correcting the slang verb phrases.

Example:　　Chiquita's gonna go to the concert next weekend.
　　　　　　Chiquita is going to go to the concert next weekend.

1.　　I wanna win a million bucks.　　(also, change the word **bucks** to **dollars**.)

_____

2.　　Tony hasta go to work at 4:00 p.m., but his brothers hafta practice piano.

_____

3.　　She's gotta learn better manners.

_____

4.　　I wanna go to Miami, because I wanna feel some sunshine.

_____

5.　　Those guys hafta eat fewer donuts, or else they're gonna get very big.

_____

6.　　We've gotta get moving, or we're gonna be late for the show.

_____

7.　　Mrs. Smith's gonna give us the grammar test because she's gotta give it.

_____

Lesson 55 — Coulda, Woulda, Shoulda   Date: _____
                        (not good)

Often when speaking, we shorten words so that we can speak more quickly.
For example, we say

shoulda	instead of	**should have**
woulda	instead of	**would have**
coulda	instead of	**could have**

The short version is fine when we are talking with friends, but when we are talking or
writing to a teacher, or a boss, or the President, it is important to use the longer forms.

A. Fill in the blanks with the correct form of the words.

1.   When Prince Charming saw that the shoe fit Cinderella's foot perfectly, he [coulda]

      _____ jumped for joy.

2.   "Cinderella! I [shoulda] _____ known it was you!"

3.   "If I hadn't escaped from the room my stepsisters locked me in, you [woulda]

      _____ never discovered the truth," replied Cinderella.

4.   "I [woulda] _____ never given up the search for you," answered
      the Prince.

B. Fill in blanks with the correct form of the appropriate verbs (beginning letters are given as
clues).

1.   "I did my homework last night, and I really **sh**_____ handed it in
      today, but my little sister ripped it up to make a bed for her hamster."
      (**would have** is also possible)

2.   "You're right, I had the chance. I didn't have to, but I **c**_____
      cleaned my room last night. I just didn't feel like it."

3.   Antonia **w**_____ started dance lessons in September if she
      hadn't broken her leg.

4.   "I **c**_____ understood what you were trying to say if you had
      spoken more clearly." (**would have** is also possible)

5.   Eduardo knew he **sh**_____ been there — he wished he had seen
      the look on Sonya's face when she found the note.

UNIT SIX   Name: _____

Lesson 56 — Using **himself, herself,**   Date: _____
              and **themselves***

When you are talking or writing about one man or one boy,
    use the word **himself.**

    Sometimes Joe talks to **himself.**   Michael Jordan **himself** came to shake my hand.

When you are talking or writing about one woman or one girl,
    use the word **herself.**

    Kathy will sing that part by **herself.**   Dolly Parton **herself** complimented Kathy.

When you are talking or writing about more than one person, use the word **themselves.**

A.   Fill in the blanks with **himself, herself,** or **themselves.**

1.   Both Mallory and Tristan spilled pop on _____ last night.

2.   My little brother Julian can walk all by _____ now.

3.   Famous people never go out in public by _____ .

4.   Then the Grinch — the Grinch _____ — carved the Roast Beast.

5.   Bonnie wrote all the invitations _____ .

6.   Freddy just wants to be by _____ today.

7.   Juanita told me _____ what happened on the weekend.

8.   Lizzie and Laura gave _____ credit for work that the whole class did.

9.   Melinda was beside _____ with joy when the new baby arrived.

10.   The President _____ is coming to visit our school!

Make up a sentence about someone in the class, using the word **himself** or **herself.**
Be sure to say something nice about them.

11.   _____

*Students, remember — "themself" is not a word! "Them" = plural; "self" = singular.

56

Name: _____

Lesson 57 — Usage: good and well   Date: _____

Many people use the word good to describe how they did on a test, or how they did during a game. They will say, "I did real good," or "I played very good."

There is a better way to say these sentences, especially when you **write** them.

Say, "I did **well** on that test," or "I played very **well**."

Use **well** as an adverb. Use **well** to describe **how something is done**.

Use **good** as an adjective. Use **good** to describe nouns — persons, places & things.

A.   Fill in the blanks with **good** or **well**.

1.   The new girl tap dances very _____ .

2.   Your new hairdo is a _____ one.

3.   The doctor says Mark's leg is healing _____ .

4.   Filling out these sentences is _____ practice for your grammar skills.

5.   With your help, I'll be a truly _____ baseball player.

6.   My dad's business isn't doing very _____ .

7.   How _____ did you brush your teeth last night?

8.   Wear your _____ shoes to your sister's wedding.

9.   You scored the winning goal! _____ for you!

10.   How _____ do you know your grandparents?

11.   Eat your carrots. They are _____ for you.

12.   I don't think they taste very _____ .

13.   Don't have a temper tantrum. What's the _____ of that?

14.   Angela does very _____ at baseball. It's not just because
       she's a _____ player, but also because she puts her heart into it.

Name: _____

Lesson 58 — Slang

Date: _____

We use the word slang to describe grammar and words that we hear all the time, but which do not sound right in a formal setting. In other words, this is not the language that we would use when we are writing our homework assignments, or when we are speaking to our teachers.

Compare paragraph number 1 to paragraph number 2. Both paragraphs mean exactly the same thing, but the first one is written in slang, and the second one in better, more formal English. Underline the changed and corrected parts in paragraph number two.

Example: (Slang)   So he goes "yeah," and I go "uh-uh, dude."
              (Corrected) So, he **said "Yes,"** and I **said, "No sir."**

Paragraph number 1:

So, didja hear about Christy and Blake? I guess they were supposta go to the movies Friday night, but he never called her. So she calls him on Saturday, and she's like, "What happened to ya on Friday night?" And he goes, "Whatcha talkin' about?" And she's like, "The movie?! Hel-lo-o?" And he just goes, "Oh, I forgot." Like, as if! Ya know what I'm sayin'? Anyways, she's all, "Whaddya mean, ya forgot?" And he's all, "Maybe we shouldn't see each other anymore." And she just goes, "What-ever!" and hangs up. So then she calls me, right? And I sez to her, I sez: "I told ya right from the start, that boy was a total jerk."

Paragraph number 2: (underline at least 10 out of the 23 parts that have been changed):

So, underline_did you hear about Christy and Blake? I guess they were supposed to go to the movies Friday night, but he never called her. So she called him on Saturday, and she asked, "What happened to you on Friday night?" He replied, "What are you talking about?" Then she said, "The movie?! Remember?" He just said, "Oh, I forgot." That's rather hard to believe, don't you agree? In any case, Christy replied, "What do you mean, you forgot?" Blake said, "Maybe we shouldn't see each other anymore." Christy simply said, "What-ever!" and hung up. Then she called me, right? I said to her: "I told you right from the start, that boy was not right for you."

Name: _____

Lesson 59 — Return of the
             Grammar Games!

Date: _____

Make funny sentences using the lists below. For example,

The _____ _____ _____ _____ _____ _____.
       ADJECTIVE   *NOUN*   *VERB*   *PRONOUN*   *NOUN*   *ADVERB*

Could become:

The   <u>ugly</u>   <u>goblin</u>   <u>teases</u>   <u>his</u>   <u>brother</u>   <u>wickedly</u>.
(or)

The   <u>crazy</u>   <u>pig</u>   <u>washed</u>   <u>his</u>   <u>cake</u>   <u>quickly</u>.

Feel free to add your own adjectives, nouns, pronouns and verbs to these lists!

ADJECTIVES	NOUNS	PRONOUNS	VERBS	ADVERBS
crazy	monkey	her	dance	quickly
special	kid	hers	eat	noisily
funny	ballerina	him	run	wickedly
ugly	brother	his	tease	strangely
clean	pig	it	wash	easily
dirty	sister	its	talk	happily
delightful	goblin		cook	peacefully
little	cake		play	mindlessly
kooky	fridge		act	eagerly
secret	friend		walk	angrily

1. My _____ pet _____ likes to _____ _____.
     ADJECTIVE   *NOUN*   *VERB*   *ADVERB*

2. I just saw a _____, and _____ was _____ing with my _____!
          NOUN   *PRONOUN*   *VERB*   *NOUN*

3. Why is that _____ _____ing so _____ ?
        NOUN   *VERB*   *ADVERB*

4. In 3000 years, the _____ _____ and the _____
               ADJECTIVE   *NOUN*   *ADJECTIVE*

_____ will be living _____ on the moon.
   NOUN   *ADVERB*

5. I can't believe Helen said that I look like a _____ and _____
                                     NOUN   *VERB*

like a _____!
     NOUN

6. Does a _____ _____ know how to _____ _____
     ADJECTIVE   *NOUN*   *VERB*   *ADVERB*

while having lunch with _____ favorite _____?
         PRONOUN   *NOUN*

A.   The following sentences contain words and phrases that you should not use when you are writing your homework or talking to teachers, parents, and presidents. Write each sentence over again, and correct all the problems.

Example: My **sister's like**, "I **hafta** go home," and her friend **goes**, "**See ya** later."

(corrected)   My **sister said**, "I **have to** go home," and her friend **replied**, "**I'll see you** later."

1. **Can** I go to the library?

_____

2. The students **hafta** fix that VCR all by **themself**.

_____

3. **Didja** hear what those girls **wanna** buy at the mall tomorrow?

_____

4. She **hasta** do **good** on her grammar test, or she's **gonna** be grounded.

_____

5. Franco is a **well** soccer player — he **done good** yesterday!

_____

6. Maria **coulda** gone to Disneyland, but she **hadda** visit her Mom.

_____

7. **Can** I **set** in this chair for a while, Mrs. Graychalk?

_____

8. **Tony's like**, "I **wanna** be the President some day, **ya** know?"

_____

9. When I heard that, I **sez**, "You've **gotta** work hard if you **wanna** succeed."

_____

Name: _____

Lesson 61 — Review: Nouns, Verbs,
**   Adjectives, Pronouns**

Date: _____

A.   Draw a line under each noun in the following sentences.

1.   The sleek red jet roared through the valley.

2.   My grandmother used to be the mayor of this city.

3.   The best movies have a lot of really good action.

B.   Draw a circle around each verb or verb phrase in the following sentences.

1.   Shania is buying herself a new dress with sequins.

2.   Rico owns a bat, Franco has a baseball, and my dad just bought a bunch of gloves.

3.   Joanie has been skateboarding all the way to school for the past three days.

C.   Draw a square around each pronoun in the following sentences.

1.   Your mother was my sister's piano teacher.

2.   As the boss of your own company, you gave yourself a big raise.

3.   My aunt and your uncle each gave her $1,000 for graduation!

D.   Draw two lines under each adjective in the following sentences.

1.   A good computer is a fast computer.

2.   At the end of the song, Garth plays a long, sad, lonely chord.

3.   A good person is fair, kind, and honest.

E.   Draw one line under each noun; a circle around each verb; a square around each pronoun; and two lines under each adjective.

1.   The quick, brown fox jumped over you and your friend!

2.   My new, orange laptop is a wonderful machine.

3.   Margarita and I went to a good concert at the Forum.

**Lesson 62 — Review: Nouns, Verbs,   Date: _____
        Adjectives, Pronouns**

A.   One word or phrase in each of the following sentences is in bold type.
      In the blank space beside each sentence, say whether that word or phrase is
      a noun, a verb, a pronoun, or an adjective.

Examples: (a) _____noun_____   Jimmy went to the **mall** with Angie.

            (b) ___adjective___   The rose is a **beautiful** flower.

1. _____   I love the **green**, green baseball fields in spring.

2. _____   Jack is one of the best **golfers** who ever lived.

3. _____   Everything **is** beautiful, in its own way.

4. _____   That Walkman belongs to **him**.

5. _____   Amber **is suffering** from a bad case of the flu.

6. _____   Terrell has an **awesome** jump shot.

7. _____   You gave **her** a wonderful present.

8. _____   Tiffany **was kicking** the soccer ball when she hurt her knee.

9. _____   **Dr. Bergen** is a wonderful dentist.

10. _____   The students did **themselves** a big favor by trying so hard!

B.   Write three of your own sentences, following the instructions in the brackets.

1. (Use two nouns. Underline both of them.) _____

_____

2. (Use two pronouns. Underline both of them.) _____

_____

3. (Use two adjectives. Underline both of them.) _____

_____

Name: _____

Lesson 63 — Words describing when, where, how

Date: _____

Adverbs can be single words describing time (when?), place (where?), and manner (how?).
When (e.g., yesterday, now. . . .)
Where (e.g., here, north. . . .)
How (e.g., quickly, quietly. . . .)

A.   Draw a line under each **one-word adverb** in the following sentences.

1.   I hope to visit my grandmother today.

2.   Most animals walk forward, but the crab seems to go sideways.

3.   Happily, they bought a whole bag full of chocolate bars.

4.   The actors in that movie spoke way too slowly.

5.   Tomorrow, our geography class plans to go on a field trip.

6.   The pioneers just kept on travelling west.

7.   A cheetah runs quickly, but a turtle waddles slowly.

8.   Tonya planned to clean her room yesterday.

9.   The racing car tilted crazily, and then it crashed.

10.   The snow starts to fall, and the birds fly south.

B.   Make up questions for each word

For example: <u>**Yesterday.**</u>
                       When did you go to the concert?

1. <u>**Now**</u>

_____ .

2. <u>**Home**</u>

_____ .

3. <u>**Smoothly**</u>

_____ .

Name: _____

Lesson 64 — Phrases describing when,
where, why, how.

Date: _____

Adverbs can also be groups of words that describe
When (e.g., "at 5 o'clock"),
Where ("in California"),
Why ("because he likes good food"),
How something happens ("in a funny way"), and
How someone travels somewhere ("by motorcycle")

A.   Draw a line under each adverb phrase.

Example: Terry watches her favorite show <u>at 4 o'clock</u> <u>in the afternoon</u>. (two time phrases)

1.   Frederico prefers to visit his grandfather on Sunday afternoons.

2.   Angelica practices her gymnastics routine in her backyard.

3.   Michael tries to stay in very good shape because he wants to win an Olympic medal.

4.   Dr. Washington always travels by train.

5.   The teachers buy lottery tickets because they want to get rich.

6.   Sylva plans to make her speech next week.

7.   Mr. Trackula walked to the corner store in a very strange manner.

B.   Make up a question for each answer.

Example: Because she wanted to rent a movie.
          <u>Why did Teresa go to the video store?</u>

1. by plane _____

_____ .

2. at midnight _____

_____ .

3. to the mountains in Colorado _____

_____ .

Name: _____

**Lesson 65 — Review of Capital Letters   Date: _____
              and Quotation Marks**

A.   Circle the letters that should be capital letters.

1.   i was talking to mr. cohen last wednesday.

2.   my best friend, jackson smith, won the high jump event on independence day.

3.   princess margaret, who lives in england, loves to visit the united states of america.

4.   brandon was born on february 29.

5.   my aunt lateesha and my uncle joe love to shop at the fairview mall.

6.   senator brown owns two houses, one in washington, d.c., and the other in boston.

B.   Put quotation marks where they belong.

1.   Billy said, I'm going to get a job in Hollywood some day.

2.   I love my old set of roller blades, Edwin said.

3.   Franco jumped up and down, shouting, Hey Marcy — I'm over here!

4.   Madeleine shouted, This is a very good grammar book!

**C.   Do two jobs — put quotation marks where they belong,
         and circle the letters that should be capital letters.**

1.   mary ann shouted loudly, i think sunday is the best day of the week!

2.   dad, may we get a cd player for christmas?   asked pedro.

3.   i want to be a famous astronaut when i grow up, tricia told mrs. fernandez.

4.   if president bush comes here, we'll all say, welcome to _____

_____ !   {name your school}

**D.   Pretend you are a writer, or a movie director. Make up the name of a very exciting
         book or movie that you would like to make. {Use capital letters properly.)**

1. _____

2. _____

UNIT SEVEN

Name: _____

Lesson 66 — Review of Commas

Date: _____

A. Put commas where they belong.

1. Shawn is having a party that starts at 7:00 p.m. Saturday July 31 2001.

2. My mother teaches university in Raleigh North Carolina.

3. Early to bed and early to rise makes someone healthy wealthy and wise.

4. My grandmother's grandmother was born on February 22 1732.

5. Deion's father just landed a job in Toronto Ontario Canada.

6. Maria what were you doing on Friday July 4?

7. Joey have you ever been to Disneyworld in Orlando Florida?

8. My sisters' names are Johanna Greta and Marian.

9. What are your favorite video games Franklin?

10. Dilip is moving to 222 Green Lane Dallas Texas.

11. The best restaurant in Kansas is The Ribeye 8 Bowie Street Kansas City.

12. The big football game starts at 2:00 p.m. Sunday October 31.

13. My three favorite movies are Return of the Jedi Jurassic Park and Phantom Menace.

14. Do you have any brothers Sarah?

15. Yes I have three. Their names are Jackson Samuel and Daniel.

16. I had a terrible day at camp Maria.

17. It was cold rainy and miserable on Friday Saturday and Sunday.

Name: _____

**Lesson 67 — Review of Contractions,
Possessives, Apostrophes**

Date: _____

A.   In the blank spaces, change the contractions into two words.

Example: ____is not____   Tammy's brother **isn't** at school today.

1. _____   Moesha's mother **hasn't** bought that new dress yet.

2. _____   **I've** wanted a new computer for two years!

3. _____   Jimmy **doesn't** like football as much as he likes baseball.

4. _____   Jena's sister said, "**Don't** go there, girlfriend!"

5. _____   The Lakers sang, "**We're** the champions of the world!"

6. _____   Sadly, the Blazers **weren't** the champions of the world.

B.   In the blank spaces, change the two highlighted words into contractions.

Example: ____isn't____   Tammy's brother **is not** feeling well.

1. _____   "**I am** not very happy with my new game," said Tyrone.

2. _____   The Jets' coach shouted, "We **have not** won anything yet!"

3. _____   The hero yelled, "**You are** not getting away, Dr. Evil!"

4. _____   The hero yelled, "You **are not** getting away, Dr. Evil!"

5. _____   Jennifer's homework **was not** on the desk.

6. _____   She **did not** know where she had last set it down.

C.   Change each singular noun to show possession. (Example: dog >> **dog's**)

Jackie   _____   hero   _____

my cat   _____   Tony   _____

sister   _____   teacher   _____

D.   Change each plural noun to show possession. (Example: actors >> **actors'**)

dolls   _____   players   _____

women   _____   children   _____

sisters   _____   teachers   _____

Name: _____

Lesson 68 — Review of Word Usage   Date: _____

A.   The following sentences contain words and phrases that you should not use when you are writing your homework or talking to teachers, parents, and presidents. Write each sentence over again, and correct all the problems.

Example: My brother **goes**, "**Ya wanna** watch TV?" and **Freddy's like**, "I **gotta** go."

(corrected) My brother said, "Do you want to watch TV?" and Freddy said, "I've got to go."

1. I really **wanna** do **good** in the game next weekend.

_____

2. There **was** a few bags of milk in the refrigerator.

_____

3. **Can me and Julio**   wipe the chalkboard tomorrow, Mrs. Rodriguez?

_____

4. Marjie **shoulda** done really **good** on her gym routine, but she tripped near the end.

_____

5. The students **hadda** mark their own tests.

_____

6. They all gave **themself** 100%!

_____

7. My grandmother always   **hasta   set**   for a few hours in that big old chair.

_____

8. Brandon's **like**, "I **hafta** get to the theater — right now!"

_____

9. **Didja** hear Jerry last night? He **goes**, "I **coulda** won a million **bucks**!"

_____

Name: _____

Lesson 69 — The Grammar Olympics!   Date: _____
(not to be confused with The Grammar Games!)

Teacher: during the following exercises, you may wish to keep score in some way, perhaps with a light touch. These games can be a lot of fun — almost too much fun. Your principal might ask, "Why was their so much laughter in your room?" — and you'll be able to reply, "We were studying grammar again!"

1.   **Nouns**. Play "I Spy," but with a variation. One student (or a student from one team) will say, "I spy something [a noun] that begins with the letter ___?___". The student who responds (or the team which responds) will get points for every noun that begins with that letter. Omit the letters X, Y, and Z from the list.

2.   **Verb Chains.** One student names a verb, then the next student names a different one, and so on. Each student has 5 seconds to think of a new verb, and has to drop out of the game if he or she has to give up. You can play this game with teams, too.

3.   **Adjective Chains.** One student names an adjective, then the next student names a different one, and so on. Each student has 5 seconds to think of a new adjective, and has to drop out of the game if he or she has to give up. You can play this game with teams, too.

4.   **Adverbs**. Play "Guess the Adverb." Ask one student (or the team) to leave the room, or to hide their eyes. The rest of the class will choose an adverb that describes how a person does something (slowly, sleepily, funnily). The student (or team) that went out of the room will then ask one student (or all the students) inside the room to do something "in the manner of the adverb." For example, they will say, "Open your book in the manner of the adverb," and the rest of the class will open their books very, very slowly. The teacher will time how long it takes students to guess the adverb.

5.   **Sentences** — the Crazy Sentence game. Each student (or each team) has to make a list of ten nouns, ten verbs, ten adjectives, and ten adverbs. Students can think of funny words when they make up their lists. Next, the teacher will put four skeleton sentences on the black board, and point to each blank with a pointer.

Example: He _____ a _____ _____ _____.
                        VERB   *ADJECTIVE*   *NOUN*   *ADVERB*
or   The _____ _____ _____ a _____ _____.
                        ADJECTIVE   *NOUN*   *VERB*   *NOUN*   *ADVERB*

The teacher points to each blank with a pointer, and asks different students each time to add a new word from their list. The teacher repeats the new, funny sentence loudly and slowly.

Lesson 70 — The Last Review (Phew!)

Name: _____

Date: _____

CROSSWORD PUZZLE

A. Find the nouns in the following sentences, then write them into their corresponding boxes.

Across 5. We're going to Jamaica

A9. The robots are out of control!

Down 1. He comes from Italy.

D5. Jimbo is so cool.

B. Find the pronouns in the following sentences, then write them into their boxes.

A3. Amy just couldn't believe it.

A8. You must write the test tomorrow.

D6. Make my day.

D7. This is our pet tarantula, Snuggles.

C. Find the verbs in the following sentences, then write them into their boxes.

A4.   There is a virus in my computer.

A12. Jennifer complains about everything.

D2.   Dial the number, please.

D10. Trap the spider under a cup!

D. Find the adverbs in the following sentences, then write them into their boxes.

A13. Let's go home.

A14. Just stay away!

D11. Ray will get what he richly deserves.

D12. Callie looked at me calmly.

ANSWER PAGES

UNIT ONE

Lesson 1
1, 3, 6, 7 >> Yes.   2, 4, 5 >> No.

Lesson 2
1. comb
2. bought
3. sings
4. has
5. owns
6. eats
7. am
8. looks like.

Lesson 4a,
A. 1. had; 2. have; 3. will have.
B. 1. was; 2. am; 3. will be.
Lesson 4b,
A. 1. liked; 2. like; 3. will like.
B. 1. liked; 2. like**s**; 3. will like.
C. 1. played; 2. play; 3. will play.

Lesson 10
A. 1. (No) <u>likes</u>
2. (Yes) <u>is</u>
3. (No) <u>wrecked</u>
4. (Yes) <u>enjoys</u>
5. (No) <u>can do</u>

B. 1. ran
2. will sing
3. looks like
4. equals
5. ate
6. will eat

UNIT TWO

Lesson 11
A..# 1, 2, 4, & 7 are whole questions.
B. # 3, 5, 6 are not whole questions.

Lesson 12
A. 1, 2, 6: sad faces.
   3, 4, 5, 7: happy faces.

Lesson 13
A. 1 (Jeremy), 5 (Lateesha),
   8 (Tyrone) >> person.
2 (Y. Park), 3 (Canada) >> place.
4 (VCR), 6 (pizza), 7 (car) >> thing.

Lesson 14
A. 1. Dad, eggs, lunch
2. Ms. Lansdowne, students,
      homework

3. Joe, game, Internet
4. Brittany, Brooklyn, shoes
5. bands, Seattle
6. Mr. Tachito, car
7. grandpa, game
8. Mrs. Pewters, fries, gravy
9. Alex, tree, house
10. mom, clothes, school.

Lesson 16
A. 1. Tuesday, July 4
2. Wednesday, December 30
3. February 22, 1732
4. 12:01 p.m., November 22, 1963
5. Saturday, January 1, 1900
6. Saturday, January 1, 2000
7. Tuesday, August 26, 1979
8. 9:30 a.m., Friday, June 2
9. July 20, 1969
10. July, 1999.

Lesson 17
A. 1. Lincoln, Nebraska
2. Versailles, France
3. Calgary, Alberta,
      Canada
4. Disneyworld, Orlando, Florida
5. 24 Goldfish Crescent,
      Nome, Alaska
6. The Steakhouse, 212 Norton
      Street, Laredo
7. Vancouver, Canada
8. Apartment 32B,
      59 Jefferson Avenue
9. Unit 10-D, 46 Appletree Lane,
      Butte, Montana
10. 22 Delaware Street,
      Washington, D.C.

Lesson 18
A. 1. big, fluffy, and warm
2. Billy-Bob, Bubba-Joe,
      and Buddy-Boy
3. graceful, agile, and flexible
4. strong, tough, and fast
5. Reading, Writing, and Arithmetic
6. long, thick, and brown
7. the Blue Jays, the Cowboys,
      and the Lakers
8. Thursday, Friday,
      and Saturday.

Lesson 20
A. Fair: 1, 3, 4.
Foul: 2, 5, 6

UNIT THREE

Lesson 21
A. 1. airplanes
2. cats   3. cakes
4. books   5. sisters
6. games   7. friends
8. donuts   9. malls.

B. 1. buses
2. passes   3. dishes
4. dresses   5. batches
6. churches   7. boxes
8. faxes   9. buzzes.

C. 1. men
2. women   3. mice
4. candies   5. halves
6. feet   7. teeth
8. geese   9. children.

Lesson 22
A. 1. child's   2. toy's
3. house's   4. cookie's
5. woman's   6. guy's
7. supermodel's 8. sandal's
9. goose's   10. father's
11. foot's   12. neighbor's
13. flower's   14. doctor's
15. teddy bear's 16. knee's
17. girl's   18. teacher's

Lesson 23
A. 1. children's
2. toys'
3. houses'
4. cookies'
5. women's
6. boys'
7. supermodels'
8. sandals'
9. geese's
10. parents'
11. feet's
12. neighbors'
13. flowers'
14.doctors'
15. teddy bears'
16. knees'
17. girls'
18. teachers'

Lesson 24
A. 1a. That is his Walkman
1b. That Walkman is his.
2a. The party was her idea.
2b. The idea for the party was hers.

B. 1a. your; b. yours.
2a. their; b. theirs.

Lesson 25
A. 1. Someone/Somebody.
2. No one/Nobody.
3. anyone/anybody.
B. 1. no one's/nobody's
2. someone's/somebody's
3. anyone's/anybody's.

Lesson 26
A. their; They; their; them; they;
they; Their; No one's/Nobody's;
my; you; your; it; him.
B. you; my; her; someone/somebody;
my; mine; it.

Lesson 27
A. The Wizard of Oz;
Batman Returns;
How the Grinch Stole Christmas;
Star Wars: Return of the Jedi

C. Anne of Green Gables;
Wonderbaby and the Flying Bathroom;
The Wind in the Willows;
The Magic Schoolbus;
Pippi Longstocking.

Lesson 28
A. 1. Freddy, do you know. . .?
2. Well, did you look . . .?
3. Yes, and it isn't there.
4. I'll bet you . . .your ear again,
   Sally, and then forgot about it.
5. No, I don't think I did. . . .
6. Well, maybe you should check.
7. Fine, Freddy, I will.
8. Oh, there it is!
9. Thank you, Freddy.
10. You're welcome, Sally.

Lesson 30
A. 1. Jimmy's; trophies
2. sisters; dogs
3. children's; movies
4. friends'; bikes: bells

B. 1(a) her; 1(b) hers
2(a) their; 2(b) theirs

C. 1(a) your; 1(b) yours
2(a) our; 2(b) ours

UNIT FOUR
Lesson 31
A. 1. knows
2. is

3. am eating
4. looks
5. was talking
6. learned
7. is planning

Lesson 32
A. 1. will be swimming
2. has been preparing
3. has been bungee-jumping
4. will travel
5. have been spying
6. has downloaded.

Lesson 33
A. 1. blue, heavy
2. yucky
3. cute
4. breezy, sunny, and warm
5. Spotted, beautiful
6. short, plaid, green and red
7. intelligent
8. tall, quick, and excellent.
9. Canadian; wild and crazy

B. 1. soft, furry, cute,
         and cuddly (or soft, furry,
cuddly, and cute)
2. small, ugly, orange.

Lesson 34
A. 1. dances; <u>shiny, red</u>
2. has; <u>curly, black</u>
3. are; <u>sweet, crunchy</u>
4. is; <u>kind, pretty</u>
5. wears; <u>soft, blue</u>
6. change, fall; <u>red, yellow</u>
7. combed, washed;
         <u>clean, tangled, dirty</u>
8. poured; <u>cold, warm</u>
9. watered, fed; <u>dry, hungry</u>
10. tripped, wished, had
   (never) left; <u>soft, cozy.</u>

Lesson 37
A. 1. Wasn't (or Isn't)
2. isn't
3. don't
4. doesn't
5. aren't
6. hasn't
7. didn't.

Lesson 38
A. I'm; She's; You're; He's;
You've; it's; they've;
you're; you're; I'm;
I'm; You're; we've.

Lesson 39

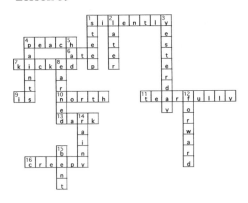

A. 1. wears; <u>new, gray</u>
2. has; <u>straight, black</u> ;
         has; <u>curly, red</u>
3. was washing; <u>dirty</u>;
         was looking; <u>dry</u>
4. will be dancing;
         <u>shiny, pointed, silver</u>
5. <u>new</u>; is; <u>fast, light, colorful</u>

C. 1. I am; she is
2. have not; they have
3. We have; will not.

UNIT FIVE
Lesson 41
A. 1, 3, 5, 8, 9 >>
         exclamation points
2, 7 >> periods
4, 6 >> question marks

Lesson 42
B. Dear; Jennifer. . . .
Thank (you). . . .
The (rash). . . .
Unfortunately, I. . . .
Lake Parleton. . .
I (remember)
However. . . .
(after) I (got hit). . . .
Please (write). . . .
I (hope)...; I (don't think) I'll....
. . . Camp Linguino. It. . . .
Your (friend), Kelly Blackett.

Lesson 45
1, 3, 4, 7, 9 >> **I**
2, 5, 6, 8 >> **me**

Lesson 46
1, 2, 5, 6, 7, 10 >> D.Q.
3, 4, 8, 9 >> I.Q.

Lesson 47
A. 1. "Does . . . skateboard?"
2. "Mom . . . Christmas?"
3. "I . . . grow up,"
4. "Hey . . . over here!"
5. "There . . . Thursday,"
6. "How . . . your foot?"
7. "I'm . . . this year,"
8. "Here's . . . birthday,"
9. "I'm sorry."
10. "I never . . . have them."

Lesson 50
A. 1. Carlos said, "I have to go to my mother's. . . lunch."
2. Gilbert shouted, "I am going to buy . . . tomorrow."
(or) "I **will buy** a new. . .tomorrow"
3. Consuela complained, "I had to do . . . last week."

B. 1. Chita thought she was going to buy herself a new dress.
2. Jim-Bob said that they have to try a lot harder if they want to win!
(or) Jim-Bob said that they <u>had</u> to try a lot harder if they <u>wanted</u> to win!
3. Every day, Tara complains that the wheels on her roller blades wear down too fast.

C. 1. . . .scolded **Billy and me....**
2. **Moesha and I saw . . . .**
3. **Frankie and I** went to the video store, but the owner told **Frankie and me** to get out!

UNIT SIX
Lesson 51
A. 1. There is a new quarter-back on . . . .
2. There was a strange light. . . .
3. There are too many vegetables on my plate.
4. There were a lot of great shows on TV. . . .
5. There is a really bad show on TV tonight.

B. 1. were
2. Was
3. was
4. were
5. are
6. Is
7. are.

Lesson 52
A. 1, 2, 6, 7, 10 >> may.
3, 4, 5, 8, 9 >> can.

Lesson 53
A. 1, 2, 3, 7 >> set
4, 5, 6 >> sit.
8 >> sitting.

Lesson 54
A. 1. want to
2. has to; have to
3. got to
4. want to; want to
5. have to; going to
6. got to; going to
7. going to; got to

Lesson 55
A. 1. could have
2. should have
3. would have
4. would have

B. 1. should have
2. could have
3. would have.
4. could have
5. should have

Lesson 56
A. 1. themselves
2. himself
3. themselves
4. himself
5. herself
6. himself
7. herself
8. themselves
9. herself
10. himself

Lesson 57
A. 1. well
2. good
3. well
4. good
5. good
6. well
7. well
8. good
9. Good
10. well
11. good
12. good
13. good
14. well; good

Lesson 58
So, <u>did you</u> (1) hear about Christy and Blake? I guess they were <u>supposed to</u> (2) go to the movies Friday night, but he never called her. So she <u>called</u> (3) him on Saturday, and she <u>asked</u> (4), "What happened to <u>you</u> (5) on Friday night?" <u>He replied</u> (6), "<u>What are you talking</u> (7) about?" <u>Then she said</u> (8), "The movie?! <u>Remember</u> (9)?" <u>He just said</u> (10), "Oh, I forgot." <u>That's rather hard to believe</u> (11), <u>don't you agree</u> (12) ? <u>In any case</u> (13), <u>Christy replied</u> (14), "<u>What do you</u> (15) mean, <u>you</u> (16) forgot?" <u>Blake said</u> (17), "Maybe we shouldn't see each other anymore." <u>Christy simply said</u> (18), "What-ever!" and <u>hung</u> (19) up. <u>Then she called</u> (20) me, right? <u>I said to her</u> (21): "I told <u>you</u> (22) right from the start, that boy was <u>not right for you</u> (23)."

Lesson 60
A. 1. May
2. have to; themselves
3. Did you; want to
4. has to; well; going to
5. good; did well
6. could have; had to
7. May; sit
8. Tony said; want to; you know
9. said; got to; want to

Lesson 61
A. **1.** jet; valley.
2. grandmother; mayor; city.
3. movies; action.

B. 1. is buying
2. owns; has; bought
3. has been skateboarding

C. 1. Your; my
2. your; you; yourself
3. My; your; her

D. 1. good; fast
2. long, sad, lonely
3. good; fair, kind, honest.

E. 1. Nouns: fox; friend
Verb: jumped
Pronouns: you; your
Adjectives: quick, brown
2. Nouns: laptop; machine
Verb: is
Pronoun: my
Adjectives: new, orange; wonderful

3. Nouns: Margarita; concert; Forum
Verb: went
Pronoun: I
Adjective: good

Lesson 62
A. 1. adjective
2. noun
3. verb
4. pronoun
5. verb
6. adjective
7. pronoun
8. verb
9. noun
10. pronoun

Lesson 63
A. 1. today.
2. forward; sideways
3. Happily
4. slowly
5. Tomorrow
6. west.
7. quickly; slowly
8. yesterday
9. crazily; then
10. south

Lesson 64
A. 1. on Sunday afternoons.
2. in her backyard.
3. because he wants to win an Olympic medal.
4. by train.
5. because they want to get rich.
6. next week.
7. to the corner store;
   in a very strange manner.

Lesson 65
A. 1. I, Mr. Cohen, Wednesday
2. My, Jackson Smith,
         Independence Day
3. Princess Margaret, England,
         United States of America
4. Brandon, February
5. My Aunt Lateesha, Uncle Joe,
         [The] Fairview Mall
6. Senator Brown, Washington, D.C.,
         Boston

B. 1. "I'm going . . . some day."
2. "I love . . . roller blades,"
3. "Hey Marcy . . . here!"
4. "This is . . . grammar book."

C. 1. Mary Ann shouted loudly, "I think Sunday is the best day of the week!"
2. "Dad, may we get a CD player for Christmas?" asked Pedro.
3. "I want to be a famous astronaut when I grow up," Tricia told Mrs. Fernandez.
4. If President Bush comes here, we'll all say, "Welcome to [name your school] !"

Lesson 66
A. 1. 7:00 p.m., Saturday, July 31, 2001.
2. Raleigh, North Carolina.
3. healthy, wealthy, and wise
4. February 22, 1732
5. Toronto, Ontario, Canada.
6. Maria, what...; Friday, July 4.
7. Joey, have...; Orlando, Florida
8. Johanna, Greta, and Marian.
9. . . . games, Franklin?
10. 222 Green Lane, Dallas, Texas.
11. The Ribeye, 8 Bowie Street, K.C.
12. 2:00 p.m., Sunday, October 31.
13. Return of the Jedi, Jurassic Park,
         and Phantom Menace.
14. . . . brothers, Sarah?
15. Yes, I. . . ; Jackson, Samuel,
         and Daniel.
16. . . . at camp, Maria.
17. . . .cold, rainy, and miserable on
         Friday, Saturday, and Sunday.

Lesson 67
A. 1. has not
2. I have
3. does not
4. Do not. . . .
5. We are . . . .
6. were not

B. 1. I'm
2. haven't
3. You're
4. aren't
5. wasn't
6. didn't

C. Jackie's; my cat's; sister's;
   hero's; Tony's; teacher's

D. dolls' ; women's:
   players' ; children's

Lesson 68
A. 1. want to; well
2. were
3. May Julio and I. . . .
4. should have; well
5. had to
6. themselves
7. has to; sit
8. Brandon said, "I have to . . . !"
9. Did you. . .; He said, "I could have
         won a million dollars!"

Lesson 70

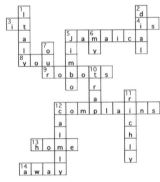

Made in the USA
Lexington, KY
15 August 2015